HAPPY BIRTHDAY DADD

FROM MARSHA

See pg. 108 for explanation
of "Equation of Time."

OLD CLOCKS

FOR MODERN USE

OLD CLOCKS

FOR MODERN USE
with a guide to their mechanism

Edward Wenham
Illustrated by Edgar Holloway

Spring Books · London

First published 1951 by G. Bell & Sons Ltd. Copyright.
This edition published 1964 by
SPRING BOOKS
Westbook House · Fulham Broadway
London
Second impression 1965

Printed in England by
Richard Clay (The Chaucer Press) Ltd.,
Bungay, Suffolk

Accurate Old Clock Based On Japanese Time System

By RALPH AND TERRY KOVEL

Confusing as they may seem to us, the beautiful old clocks that the Japanese developed and used until about 1870, when the European time-telling method of the 60-minute hour was adopted, did keep accurate time. However, it is important for us to realize that the early clocks were based on a time system that had nothing to do with our present system.

The day was divided into two major parts—sunset to sunrise, and sunrise to sunset. Each of these was divided into six parts, with midnight or midday always the ninth hour on the clock. The other time parts of the day could vary in length.

Japanese clocks were made with adjustable hour and half-hour markers and with a single hand which traveled backward by our standards.

Clock Used Until 1870

PREFACE

IN A BRIEF FOREWORD to his lurid autobiography, a gangster wrote, 'I have never had any use for prefaces unless they told me something that mattered and helped me understand what came afterwards'—in the picturesque language of his kind, a preface was a 'flat tire', empty and useless.

Convention more or less demands that a book should open with a brief address to introduce the reader to what it's all about, though we writers are apt to forget this and allow ourselves to start on a merry-go-round of irrelevancies. After which admission, heed must here be paid to the suggestion of our underworld author to say 'something that matters'.

In the following chapters, the story of time and time-tellers is that which the writer has learned largely from the enjoyment of a restful hobby over the years. That story should be of interest to all those who have an affection for fine clocks, whether old or modern, as part of their home surroundings; and furthermore, it should offer hints and helps to those (mostly men) who retain their youth-time joy of 'tinkering' with machinery.

Most of us whose daily task is of a sedentary character can, in our spare time, enjoy a sense of freedom from the monotony of that daily round by using our hands on some little piece of machinery and so giving our head a rest. Few hobbies calling for the use of tools demand less physical effort and, at the same time, afford a real sense of accomplishment than that of restoring a dormant clock to activity. And it is hoped that this book will be as productive of as much constructive amusement for others as the writer has known and still knows from ministering to the needs of some dilapidated and discarded timepiece.

Every effort has been made to avoid technical jargon in describing and explaining the various parts of different movements. Where recognized terms of the clockmaker's craft have been used, the equivalent in 'layman's language' has been given—though we amateurs are always proud if we can talk the 'professional' lingo.

When a desire to dabble in the pleasant pastime of playing at clockmaking first makes itself felt, it is well to remember that, to the uninformed, any piece of machinery can appear almost alarmingly intricate; but if it is studied 'bit by bit' and the reason for its action and movement followed to the source, its mystery disappears and is replaced by the pleasure which comes from understanding. This applies especially to a clock movement which may be examined in all its details at leisure moments.

Nor does an amateur need any large workshop. All he requires is a small bench or fairly firm table in a corner with adequate light and the relatively few tools of the trade which are quite small, apart from a lathe which itself is not large. Maybe the first attempts at 'making a clock tick' are not immediately successful; but patience and perseverance, invariably stimulated by the fascination exercised by any clock movement, will bring the looked-for result.

As with all delicate crafts, working on a clock demands the constant application of the old adage, 'Hasten slowly'. He who aspires to become a 'horological surgeon' must recognize fully the sound advice in those two words. The slower he works at the job when he starts to learn, the more he will observe and learn concerning the anatomy of the patient, the sounder will be his diagnosis and the greater the hope for success when he undertakes any serious operation.

Sundials and other ancient recorders of the passing hours have been described and illustrated and 'recipes' given for making some of the simpler types; these should offer no difficulty to any with a mechanical bent—certainly less than to our primitive ancestors who had to contrive the originals, whereas we have merely to copy the models.

Various novel time-tellers which, at different periods, were invented by individual men of whom many were amateurs have been described and illustrated. These are well worth studying especially by those endowed with inventiveness, because it is probable some will suggest possible improvements on the original idea while others are well within the ability of present-day amateurs to reproduce. In that same chapter, reference is made to the association of clocks to perpetual motion which, too, offers wide scope for experiment. It will be seen from the descriptions and illustrations that several inventors, including the Marquis of Worcester, evolved unusual forms of time-recorders which would suggest these men were seeking some means to achieve perpetual motion.

A list of some four thousand clockmakers and the date at which each became a member of the Worshipful Company of Clockmakers has been included. While such a list is of primary importance in ascertaining the period at which a clock was made (where the maker's name is known), it should be emphasized that, as there were men of the same name who lived and worked at the craft at often widely separated periods, various details such as the dial, hour ring, hands etc. have to be taken into consideration—these details are described in Chapter Thirteen. To here quote one example: From the granting of the Clockmakers' Charter in 1631 until the end of the following century, there were eight men named John Harris who were freemen of the Company of Clockmakers.

Names of others who worked at the trade but were not freemen are to be found in books dealing specifically with the clockmakers of various countries—*Watchmakers and Clockmakers of the World*, by G. H. Baillie, is a work of this character.

That sense of obligation which every writer must know to many is perhaps unusually widespread in connexion with the present book. Opinions regarding the minor queries that invariably crop up have been freely given by those to whom they were addressed. Similarly, photographs and other illustrative matter have been forthcoming from those engaged in handling fine clocks, with that spontaneity which this writer has known for long and which he has never failed to appreciate.

In this connexion, the gratitude expressed in previous books to members of the British Antique Dealers' Association is here repeated to: Messrs. E. T. Biggs & Sons, Ltd. (Maidenhead), William Bruford & Son, Ltd. (Exeter), Christie, Manson and Woods, Ltd., The Goldsmiths and Silversmiths Company, Ltd., Judge Jeffreys' Lodgings (Dorchester), Ronald A. Lee (Richmond Hill), Mallett & Son (Antiques), Ltd., Phillips of Hitchin, Ltd.,

Alexander Podd (Dunstable), A. T. Silvester & Sons, Ltd. (Birmingham) and Charles E. Thornton (Petergate).

This affords me an opportunity to put on record my obligation to my friend Stephen J. Jussel of Arthur S. Vernay, Inc., New York, both for his generous help in furnishing photographs for this book and for equally generous help on other occasions.

Information relating to and photographs of specimens in our public collections have, as always, been made available and my appreciation of their several responses to my requests is expressed to the Curators of the Ashmolean, the British, the Guildhall, the Science and the Victoria & Albert Museums.

Drawings for illustrating the section on modern clocks have been made from actual movements and photographs loaned by different houses. The movements in (66) and (70) were loaned by Messrs. Andrew & Co., Ltd.; that in (65) by The Bentima Co., Ltd.; (13) by Ernest A. Watkins, Ltd., and photographs of others were furnished by The Goldsmiths and Silversmiths Co., Ltd., and Rotherham & Sons, Ltd., Coventry.

For their patient courtesy in complying with my rather persistent inquiries I am especially sensible of my indebtedness to Messrs. E. Pitcher & Co. and particularly to Mr. M. A. Pitcher of that firm who has allowed me to occupy his time freely, when discussing modern reproductions of early clocks.

A list of the various private collectors who have kindly replied to my questions concerning their clocks would be somewhat lengthy. I would, however, voice my sincere thanks to Mr. Frederick R. Poke for allowing me to illustrate some of the fine clocks which are in his collection; and also to Mr. Edgar Allen of Westbury on Trym, Bristol, for permission to include specimens from his collection.

My thanks are expressed to the Editor of the *Western Morning News* for the privilege of illustrating the historical clock on the Church of St. Mary at Steps, Exeter (XVII).

Acknowledgement to the Worshipful Company of Clockmakers and to Mr. Raymond Smith, the Librarian of the Guildhall Library for their invaluable assistance in compiling the list of clockmakers is made in Chapter Sixteen.   E. W.

CONTENTS

SECTION 5

THE FEATURES WE SEE

SECTION 6

THE NEW FROM THE OLD

SECTION 7

THROUGH THREE CENTURIES

THE LINE ILLUSTRATIONS

THE PHOTOGRAPHS

These photographs appear between pages 80 and 81.

SECTION 1
Primitive Time-tellers

CHAPTER ONE

SUNDIALS

LIKE THE BEGINNING of time itself, man's first efforts to record the passing hours of life are lost behind the curtain of the untraceable past. One of the earliest references to time measurement occurs in the second Book of Kings, 'and he [the Lord] brought the shadow ten degrees backward, by which it had gone down in the dial of Ahaz'; and King Ahaz lived about twenty-seven hundred years ago.

Curiosity has always fostered discovery. Thus when primitive man first noticed that the position of his shadow changed, during the period of daylight, he became interested in the reason. Then he noticed that his shadow or that of any other object was long at sunrise, became shorter and shorter and later lengthened with the approach of darkness; and so he learned that the length and position of a shadow were controlled by the position of the sun.

We may assume that eventually he conceived the idea of stripping the branches from a small tree, fixed the stem in an open space and marked the length of the shadow and the place where it fell at different intervals during the time the sun was shining. In this way, he learned both to divide day from night and the day into more or less definite periods of time. This was the first form of the so-called shadow-clocks or what we know as the sundial.

Shadow-clocks and sundials were in common use by the ancient Babylonians and Egyptians, and in the Science Museum, South Kensington, there is a copy of an Egyptian shadow-clock from an original of nearly 3,000 years ago, which is (or was) in the Neues Museum, Berlin.

This quite simple object is rather like a draughtsman's **T**-square, but the cross-bar of the **T** has a short 'tail' set vertically (on its edge as it were) at right angles with the long section along which the shadow of the cross-bar, changing with the sun, gradually moved and indicated the time of the day (1).

1. Reproduction of the earliest known shadow-clock. Egyptian, tenth to eighth century B.C. In the Science Museum. The cross piece is conjectural

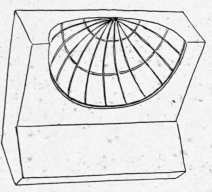

2. Roman hemicycle divided into twelve parts of the day. The gnomon (omitted in the illustration) was at the point from which the twelve lines radiate

Smith, in his *Dictionary of Greek and Roman Antiquities,* quotes the two earliest and simplest time indicators invented by the Babylonians. These were actually sundials and the day was divided into twelve parts. The more ancient of the two was a perpendicular pole (gnomon) set up in a sunny position and the shadow of this was measured in feet on the place where the shadow fell; the longest shadow at sunrise and sunset being 12 feet. The other more advanced sundial known as a 'polos' or hemicycle, was a half-basin shape hollowed from a block of stone (2). The inside surface was divided into twelve parts of the day by lines radiating from the point where a perpendicular staff or gnomon was fixed, the shadow of which thrown by the sun indicated the hour—the gnomon is omitted from the illustration.

From this and other ancient time-tellers we derived the various forms of vertical sundials still to be found on old churches and

3. Type of sundial used in gardens. It is divided to show the minutes and a graduated circle within the hour circle indicates the corresponding 'equation of time' for converting solar to mean time. By William Deane, 1718

Science Museum

other buildings, and those attractive ornaments in old-time gardens (3). And many churches in this country dating from Tudor times and before, still have the simple time indicators known as scratch-dials.

These were miniature sundials which were scratched at eye level on the south wall of country churches during the Middle Ages. Traces of the radiating lines and of the hole where the gnomon was fixed are still to be found on the walls of many hundreds of churches throughout the country and occasionally on barns and other buildings. An interesting pamphlet on the subject by T. W. Cole is listed among others in the bibliography.

In that delightful miscellany, *The Book of Days*, reference is made to Joseph Moxon's (1659) directions for making various types of sundials including 'a solid ball or globe that will show the hour of the day without a gnomon.' The globe was marked round the 'equator' with two series of numbers, 1 to 12. It was so placed that one 12 o'clock was to the north and the other to the south, so that when the sun shone on the globe, the number at the point where the shadowed part met the lighter part denoted the hour of the day (4).

This description is accompanied by an illustration of a globular dial fixed on the top of a classical column with several figures at the base and a drinking fountain on each side of the plinth; and the remarkable sundial and fountain is described as 'formerly at Leadenhall Corner, London' where it was erected by John Leak 'in the mayoralty of Sir John Dethick, knight...'

Jacques, in *As You Like It*, remarks,

> And then he drew a dial from
>   his poke
> And looking on it with lack-
>   lustre eye
> Says, very wisely, 'It is ten
>   o'clock.'

4. Moxon's globular sundial, said to have been at Leadenhall Corner

This was a pocket dial (sometimes called poki-dial) such as was in common use in Shakespeare's day and later. It was a shallow cylinder about two inches diameter, not unlike a plain table napkin ring, suspended by a small loop similar to that of a modern pocket watch. A tiny conical-shaped hole was drilled in the side and when the ring was held with the hole toward the sun, the rays passing through the hole made a spot of light on the inside surface which was marked with the daylight hour numerals. Later ring dials (to use the generally accepted name) were fitted with a sliding ring, technically called a cursor, in which the hole was drilled and these could be adjusted to the latitude and season of the year (5).

Another simple 'clock' was the shadow of a wall or other vertical falling upon one or more fixed marks; and this survived until fairly recent times in country districts where a mark was made on a window sill and when the shadow touched that mark, the goodwife knew it was time for dinner.

Incidentally, there is little difficulty and a considerable sense of pleasurable achievement in making a sundial. The writer has made several and here are the 'recipe' and the necessary tools; A piece of slate or sandstone about 16 inches square—this should be quite smooth on one side and any thickness more than an inch; a short piece of galvanized wire about one-eighth inch in diameter, and a carpenter's pencil. From your favourite carpenter, you can borrow a pair of dividers (the kind with strong metal points such as can be used for scribing stone); a brace with a one-eighth inch drill; a spirit level; and a square. The reason for slate or sandstone is that each of these is relatively soft and easy to drill and score.

Mark deeply with the point of the dividers on the slate or stone a circle about 14 inches diameter and, inside that, another circle about 12 inches diameter. Mark the centre clearly and carefully with the point of the dividers. On that exact centre, drill a hole about one inch deep. Then cut a piece, about 9 inches, of the galvanized wire and be sure this is perfectly straight.

Place the piece of slate or stone where it is to remain and where it is in the sun for as many hours as possible. See that the base on which you put it (ours is let into the ground on a lawn) is quite firm and then make sure the top or face of the slate is level in all directions by testing with the spirit level. After that, run a little fairly wet cement in the hole drilled in the centre and push the piece of wire into the hole tapping it lightly to 'seat' it. The next and last operation is to see that the wire is quite perpendicular and this you test with the square—the wire will fit snugly enough to allow its being moved slightly before the cement has set.

On an evening when the sun sinks red in the west and you have a free day to follow, arrange for an early breakfast and watch where the first shadow of the piece of galvanized wire falls on the stone at an hour or half-hour. Rule along this shadow with a carpenter's pencil—this makes a broader mark than an ordinary pencil. From then, at each half-hour by your watch, mark the shadow until evening—you will probably be able to do this until about 8 o'clock (summer time).

You will find that after the first morning shadow you pencil in, each successive one will be slightly shorter until noon which is the shortest (that is 1 o'clock summer time). After noon, the shadows lengthen again and by evening will be as long as they were in the morning. It is well to pencil the time against each of the shadow lines you draw to mark the hours and half-hours.

Later you can, with some sharp tool and a rule, score in the pencilled lines—do this fairly deeply. When doing this, let the radiating lines end at the inner circle. Then you can either cut in or paint the hours in roman figures between the two circles and show the half-hours by a fleur-de-lys or a lozenge or even a bold dot—if you feel you are not sufficiently adept at drawing roman figures, enlist the help of a friend with more experience. And you can, of course, add another circle in which the corresponding 'summer time' hour may be shown in arabic figures.

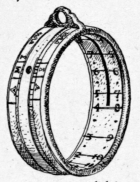

5.   Pocket ring sundial in use
from the early fifteenth century

Science Museum

CHAPTER TWO

WATER AND SAND TIME-RECORDERS

TIME-TELLERS KNOWN AS clepsydrae (Greek for stealer of water) which measured time by a gradual trickle of water were first used to regulate the time allowed for speeches in the courts at Athens and later were in fairly common use among the ancient Greeks and Romans. They were by no means good timekeepers, however, and had to be rectified frequently during the daylight hours by the time registered on the more reliable sundial.

But they may be regarded as the ancestor of the much later mechanical clocks because some of them were fitted with a dial and an indicator which was controlled by a pulley and a weight, or other means, many centuries before the introduction of the timekeepers that were recognized as clocks, as we know them.

Time-recorders which registered the passing of time by means of water belong to two categories: the earlier simple bowl or other shaped vessel, and those of the more advanced type with some mechanical device. A fair number of Egyptian examples which have been found are similar in shape to an ordinary tapered flower-pot. These were filled with water which leaked from a small hole in the side at the bottom, the flow of the leak being regulated by the size of the hole.

This shape was adopted for the reason that when the vessel was full the width at the top counter-balanced the greater pressure of water; and, as the level of the water became lower and the pressure decreased, so the tapering shape decreased the surface of the water, thus ensuring a more or less uniform leakage through the hole. And as the water fell, so it exposed a scale of the hours which were shown on the inside of the vessel. A cast of this type of water clock is in the Science Museum, South Kensington.

Other similarly primitive time-tellers operated in reverse to the one described. A bowl or basin filled with water was fitted with a tiny spout, the water dropping from this into another vessel which was marked with the hours of both day and night. In other instances a bronze bowl with a tiny hole in the bottom was floated on water in another vessel. After a certain interval, which was relatively constant, the bowl sank and a watcher would mark the time by striking a bell, a means of registering time used by our Saxon ancestors in Britain.

Another method was by filling a fairly long glass tubular vessel with water which trickled through a tiny opening at the bottom into a container. The tube was fixed vertically on a tripod and the side marked with the hours starting with 1 at the top and continuing downward to 12. With this type of water clock, the gradations of the hours decrease downward. Thus between 1 and 2 the space is greater than between 2 and 3 and so on until 10, 11 and 12 are close together. This is explained by the fact that when the tube was full, the pressure was greater and so more water leaked away, but as the level of the water became lower so the pressure decreased and the water dripped more slowly.

Another equally simple water clock recorded the time by a float connected to a syphon which drew the water from the container. And with this kind the pressure was constant and the hour markings on the side were equidistant one from the other; any necessary regulating being done by adjusting a small tap on the end of the syphon by which the flow of the water could be increased or decreased.

Several types of time recorders with a dial and a pointer worked by water were made in quite early times. And it is possible to trace the addition of mechanical devices which, strictly speaking, were the forerunners of some of the later 'inventions'.

With one type devised by the Egyptians, a continuous flow of water was fed through a small pipe into a funnel from which it dripped into a tall cylindrical vessel below; the rate of the intake flow being controlled by a stopper shaped to fit the funnel, to the top of which a tiny overflow pipe was attached. A float fixed to a stout rod with a series of teeth (called a rack) on the upper part was the actual 'driving power'. As the level of the water rose, the float also rose and pushed the rod upward and the teeth engaged with other teeth on a small wheel slowly turning this small wheel to which was fixed a pointer indicating the hours on a dial. To 'wind' this clock, the cylindrical vessel was emptied, the float then dropping down to start its upward journey again as the cylinder refilled.

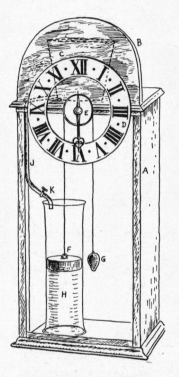

6. Modern adaptation of an ancient clepsydra or water clock with a float and a counterweight

7. One-hour sand-glass of two bulbs joined in a wooden frame

While the dial of this ancient time-teller was similar to one of the present day, in that it was marked with the hours I to XII, the hour figures appeared twice on the dial: once on the half of the hour circle which shows I to VI on modern clocks and again on the other half which nowadays shows the hours VII to XII.

Another ingenious contrivance, in which the toothed rod and wheel were replaced by a float and counterweight was fitted with an intricate device for adjusting the flow of water; and some few years ago, the writer aspired to make a simplified form of this type of clepsydra.

In case some reader might care to emulate this effort, here are the 'ingredients' as shown in (6). Make a small wood frame, similar to a shallow box with the top and bottom removed (A); it should be about 12 inches long and 4 inches deep. To the front side of one end (the end which is to be the top) add a fairly deep wide arch of a piece of figured wood (B), the purpose of the arch being to conceal the tank or reservoir (C). From a piece of tin cut out a hollow circle for the dial or hour ring, paint this white and later add the hour figures (D). If you are not sufficiently skilled with a pair of shears, a tinsmith will cut out the hour ring; and should your ability with a small brush be, like this writer's, somewhat immature, a more artistic friend will paint the roman numerals for you.

For the working parts you need a small pulley (E); a single clock hand, a piece of light chain (or heavy catgut) and a float (F); a small lead weight (G); a beaker (H); and the reservoir (C); for the last you will need further help from your tinsmith, unless you are fairly skilled in metal work.

Obviously the hand or pointer must be fixed to the pulley, for which reason we used a wood pulley. To fix the hand, drill two quite small holes and fasten it with tiny screws to the pulley. For a float, you can use a circular piece of hardwood of a size only slightly smaller than the diameter of the beaker; the lead counter-weight should exactly balance the float when both are hanging free from the chain or catgut over the pulley, so that as the water rises in the cylindrical vessel the weight 'takes up the slack' and turns the pulley—our 'cylindrical vessel' was a straight-sided flower vase from among the family possessions.

Using the knowledge of the Egyptians, we made the 'tank' or reservoir the shape of a flower-pot, but with the bottom slightly slanting toward the hole in the side at the bottom. From this hole a very small tube (J) carried the water along the top of and down the inside of the frame to a tiny tap (K) from which it was led into the lower container. This little tap allows the flow of water to be varied and 'regulates' the clock. No claim is made that the pointer of this twentieth-century clepsydra synchronizes with the 'pips', but it was a lot of fun making it and at least it is quaintly ornamental.

Incidentally, if at any time you find a similar contrivance in some 'Ye Olde', do not imagine you have discovered an ancient relic—you have merely come on a modern copy or adaptation. But it might be remarked that water was used as the driving power of time-tellers until the end of the seventeenth century.

In his book on American clocks, Carl Drepperd refers to sand clocks which were made in the United States during the second half of the eighteenth and the first half of the nineteenth centuries. He describes the 'movement' as a spindle, a length of cord wound around it and a heavy ball resting in a large box of sand. The sand, permitted to escape, lowered the heavy ball, which unwound the cord and turned the spindle; hence the hands turned and told the 'time'.

When sand-glasses (7) were first used for measuring time is part of history lost in the mists of the past; but they are still familiar in present-day homes—if not for recording the passing hours at least to record the passing minutes when boiling an egg and, we believe, other culinary pastimes. Probably one of their uses through many centuries and one which survived, to some extent, until relatively recent times was as a form of restraint on the loquacity of bygone parsons when they delivered their homilies from the pulpit.

In the Bishop's Bible, printed in 1569, there is an illustration of Archbishop Parker with an hour-glass standing by his side. There are references to these ecclesiastical 'remembrancers' in early church inventories where they are described as 'One whole houre-glasse' or 'One halfe houre-glasse' denoting that the parson was permitted a long or shorter time in which to discourse. These glasses were placed either on the side or in a bracket in front of the pulpit and though fewer of the glasses with their sand remain complete, a number of the original iron brackets are to be seen in various churches in this country.

At the commencement of his sermon, the preacher turned the glass and his prolixity was measured and regulated by the sand as it ran from the top to the bottom bulb. And there are various amusing accounts of the strategy used by early divines to circumvent the 'running out of the sand'. It is told of Daniel Burgess, the noncomformist preacher, that in one of his harangues against strong drink, the sand had run out of the glass long before he had exhausted his vehemence. Placing his hand on the hour-glass, he said, 'Brethren, I have more to say on the nature and consequences of drunkenness, so let's have another glass.'

If our memory serves, the reverend gentleman had borrowed this from an earlier engraving of that ecclesiastical buffoon, Hugh Peters.

8.   Lamp which indicated the hours of the night by the level of the oil in the reservoir

Science Museum

CHAPTER THREE

TIME BY FIRE, CANDLE AND LAMP

STRICTLY SPEAKING, 'Candle and Lamp' might have been omitted
from the title of this chapter, but they are included for the sake of
classification. The fire method of noting the passing of time
consisted of setting alight to some material, such as hemp treated
so that it would smoulder, and marking it at specific places to
indicate equal periods. This may be illustrated by lighting a dry
wick of a pocket lighter and blowing out the flame—from a test
in fairly still air we made before suggesting that illustration half
an inch of wick was consumed in $2\frac{1}{2}$ minutes and again using
1 inch of wick the time was 5 minutes. From that, it seems
apparent that the smouldering is fairly constant. Perhaps some
mathematician will compute how large a wick of the same
material is necessary to smoulder for an hour.

When man learned that a wick in the middle of some fatty
substance would give light and so invented the candle, he
noticed that it was consumed slowly, and he then began to see its
possibilities as a primitive time measure.

There is in the (so-far unauthenticated) life of Alfred the
Great by Asserius Menevensis, the ninth-century monk, a detailed
description of Alfred's use of candles as time-tellers. According
to this, six candles were used daily, each one being twelve inches
long and as each contained over three quarters of a pound of wax
(probably beeswax and tallow), these would be fairly large. The
length was marked off into twelve equal divisions, three of which
would burn for one hour, which meant that each candle lasted for
four hours. As one burned to its end, another was lighted so that
the six carried through the twenty-four hours.

This same account tells us that to counteract the draughts
which whistled through the chinks in the walls of his chapel or
the opening of his tent, King Alfred designed lanterns of thin
layers of ox horn fitted into wooden frames to ensure the 'candle
clocks,' burning with greater regularity. If the work of Asserius

should be proved genuine, then he credited Alfred with various innovations which were known many centuries before his time. Lanterns with horn sides were used by the ancient Greeks and Romans and it is highly probable that measuring time by candle was known long before Alfred adopted it.

There was a revival of 'candle clocks' about a century ago. Candles were made either with marks round the sides or different colouring at regular intervals, according to the size of the candle. These divisions denoted hours, half-hours and quarter-hours and so indicated the time as the candle burned. And time-measuring candles are still made by Price's Patent Candle Company for use by the Science Museum.

Candles marked down the side with divisions indicating a particular period of time were used in the old custom of 'auction by inch of candle'. This custom belongs to the days when life was far slower than it is now and when money was not such a powerful influence. At an auction sale an inch of candle was lighted and a lot went to the person who bid last before the wick fell; or a pin would be pushed into the side of a lighted candle one inch from the top and the bidding continued until the candle burned down sufficiently and the pin dropped into the tray of the candlestick, when the lot was knocked down to the last bidder. And in Chapter Eleven we describe an eighteenth-century quaint time-teller on a similar principle to a sundial, but replacing the sun by a candle.

There is evidence, too, that oil lamps were used by ancient peoples as time measurers and these continued popular in parts of Europe until fairly recent times. They consist of a glass reservoir on a stem and foot rather like a candlestick, and are usually of pewter. A small lamp-like wick holder is fixed just below the reservoir which is held in place by two vertical strips of pewter. One of these strips is marked with the hours in roman numerals, the time being indicated by the level of the oil in the reservoir which naturally falls lower as it is consumed by the burning wick. The order of the numerals on the pewter strip varies with different examples, but always includes the hours of darkness at any period of the year (8).

SECTION 2
The First Mechanical Clocks

CHAPTER FOUR

WEIGHTS AND WHEELS

LIKE ANY OTHER machine, a clock depends upon driving power and proper control of that power to perform its purpose satisfactorily. And after its introduction, in about 1660, the pendulum was fitted to time-tellers which were driven by water pressure; but while water clocks continued to be made until the time of William and Mary, we are, here, concerned more with the familiar kind dependent upon weights, springs and wheels which, when they first appeared, were known as 'artificial clocks'—'artificial' denoting that they were made by human hands and not the more generally accepted meaning, i.e. imitation.

To most people, a clock is a dial which shows the time and advises us when we should do some certain thing, and says 'tick-tick' or 'tick-tock' according to its size. Some of us remember that it needs winding occasionally, otherwise it is perhaps regarded merely as ornamental and possibly with some degree of sentiment as something that has come down through several generations of the same family.

But a fine clock is much more. It represents the aggregation of man's inventions through the centuries in achieving mechanical movement. Moreover, with some understanding of the, actually simple, inter-working of the various wheels, it is possible to trace what might be called the embryonic forms of the powerful machinery which was evolved in later years.

Incidentally, the word 'clock' is our form of the old English *clokke*, the Latin *clocca* and the old French *cloque* each of which means a bell. In bygone days, the hour shown on the sundial was indicated by sounding a bell. The later French form of the word, *cloche*, still strictly denotes a bell-shaped glass for placing over plants in a garden, though it is now applied to any shape of these valuable gardening helps.

Without indulging in the many technical minutiae, it is possible to gain sufficient understanding of how and why the hands of a clock go round the circle and what makes it tick. And as the long case or grandfather with an eight-day movement is more widely familiar, and, what is more important, it is possible to lift off the hood and see the works we will use it as the 'object lesson'; but if you take off the hood to see the works, it's wise to recall that little notice in museums, 'Do Not Touch'.

Any explanation of a set of clock works usually begins at the top and continues downward, but, here we will ignore precedent, because to most of us, there is more interest if one has a general idea of what makes a machine move, before giving any study to what it moves.

In any striking clock, like our grandfather, the various inter-working wheels connected with its time-recording and those which cause it to strike the hours are each known as a 'train'; and this always seems an apt word, because like a railway train it is composed of a number of separate, but interdependent members motivated by the same power—and again like a railway train, if any one part of it develops a fault, the whole stops moving.

All clocks derive their motive power either from a pull or a push. Our eight-day grandfather is kept going by the pull of a heavy weight hooked to a small pulley wheel suspended by a catgut line from a drum or barrel on which the line is coiled when the clock is wound up. One end of the axle (technically the arbor) of the drum extends to the dial and forms the winding square which fits the key and at the other there is a fairly heavy toothed wheel, with a smaller toothed wheel fixed on the inside. The latter does not concern us as it is merely the ratchet-wheel which prevents the drum turning in the opposite direction when winding up the weight. The larger wheel, however, is of primary importance because it is the great or driving wheel.

As the pull of the weight turns the drum and so turns the great wheel, the latter engages a tiny cogwheel with a small number of teeth or leaves (called a pinion) on the arbor (axle) of a wheel known as the centre wheel. The arbor of the centre wheel passes through the dial and the long or minute hand is fastened to the square end.

This centre wheel engages another tiny wheel (pinion) above it and this in turn drives what is called the second wheel which has slightly fewer teeth than the centre wheel. This second wheel again engages a small wheel (pinion) above it and in so doing turns the one known as the escape-wheel; the escape-wheel is the one at the top which is stopped momentarily and then allowed to move again by the anchor-like gadget that rocks from side to side with the swing of the pendulum which is suspended on a thin spring. The arbor (axle) of this wheel extends to the dial and carries the small pointer which registers the passing of the seconds on a little dial.

All the wheels so far mentioned are between the front
and back plates which are held
together by four turned brass
pillars. Other wheels, referred
to as the 'motion work' (9)
are placed between the front
plate and the dial. One of
these rides on the extended
arbor (axle) of the centre
wheel, described above, and
turns the hand recording the
minutes—that is, it makes a
complete round of the circle
once in an hour.

This minute-recording
wheel engages with one called

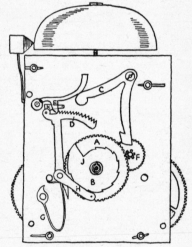

9. Motion work of an eight-day clock, the details of which are described in this chapter

the reversed hour or motion wheel to which is fixed a pinion with six leaves (cogs) and this drives a large wheel with seventy-two teeth (A); in other words the latter revolves once in twelve hours (72 divided by 6) and so turns the 'pipe' on which the hour hand is carried. In front of this hour wheel and fixed to the pipe there is an odd looking notched plate, or cam, similar in shape to a snail and is in fact known as the 'snail' (B), which as we shall see controls the striking.

On the other side of the clock, between the plates, there are another winding barrel with a driving wheel, a series of wheels and pinions and a small fan-fly. These form the striking train and are driven by a weight similar to that described above. The driving wheel engages a pinion fixed to the arbor of a wheel which has eight pins on the rim and as the latter turns, each of the pins 'trips' the tail of and raises the hammer. The hammer is controlled by a spring which, by an ingenious shaping of the end of the shank (the arm carrying the hammer head), impels the hammer on to the gong after the tail is raised and, at the same time, prevents its hitting the gong with too much force.

As the pin wheel turns, it engages a pinion of a wheel above it, the last engaging a pinion of a third wheel which, in turn, engages a pinion on the arbor of the fan-fly; and as, in this instance a wheel of forty-eight teeth drives a small cogwheel of seven leaves (pinion), the fan-fly whizzes round and, by its resistance to the air, acts as a brake to regulate the speed of the train. Other pieces connected with the striking are between the front plate and the dial and are in addition to the wheels and snail already referred to—to use their technical names, a lifting piece (C), a rack (D), a rack hook or click (E) and a gathering pallet (K).

This is how these oddly shaped pieces 'co-operate' to make the clock strike: As the long or minute hand turns, so, as explained, the motion or reversed wheel (F) is turned; and as the minute hand approaches XII, it brings a small pin on the side of the motion wheel against the tail of the inverted L-shaped lifting piece (C). The minute hand as it advances to XII continues to push the pin against the lifting piece until the upper arm raises the rack hook out of the teeth of the rack (D).

This at once releases the rack which, pushed by the spring at its tail (G), falls to the left and it is then you hear the 'warning' as it is called. The distance (actually the number of teeth) the rack is allowed to move is controlled by the position of the snail against which the tail at the bottom of the rack (H) falls; in other words, the deeper the tail falls into the snail, the greater the number of hours to be struck on the bell. Thus, for instance, at 12 o'clock the tail reaches the deepest part of the snail, i.e. the right angle (J) but at one o'clock it is 'brought up short' by the top of the vertical and each subsequent hour it meets with a lower notch or step.

When the minute hand actually reaches XII, the pin on the motion wheel passes the tail of the lifting piece which then drops and allows the point of the rack hook to fall into the teeth of the rack and the train is then free. A small rotating tooth known as the gathering pallet picks up a tooth of the rack each time the striking wheel lifts the hammer and so 'pulls' the rack back to the right until the turning of the gathering pallet is stopped by a pin at the left hand end of the rack.

CHAPTER FIVE

THE PULSE OF TIME

EVERYTHING THAT MOVES, either of its own volition or mechanic-ally, has some part of it which may be called the heart from which the impulses spring. Moreover, such things each give forth a more or less audible repetitive two-beat sound similar to that which in human and other animals is called a pulse. A steam engine will give out a puff-puff or a double sighing sound; that of a pump is similar; it can be heard in the action of a motor car piston and in other machinery.

So with a clock, the escapement is the heart and the 'tick-tock' might be called the sound of the pulse. As a human, without a working heart, could not live, a clock without an escapement would 'run down' immediately, for the reason that as soon as the weight was wound up, it would fall again as quickly as the various wheels of the movement could whizz round.

Therefore, before a satisfactory mechanical clock movement could be ensured, it was essential that some form of check should be found which, while resisting the pull of the weight on the wheels, would not interfere with their smooth and regular movement. And here, we will betake ourselves for a while along the path of the past to the time when the early clock-makers began to discover some means of ensuring this and to follow the subsequent inventions and improvements which gave us the splendid timepieces of the late seventeenth century and since.

Little is actually known of the development of mechanical clocks before the fourteenth century and that little is largely speculative. The earliest examples that have been preserved are large public clocks of iron with what is called the verge escape-ment, of which there are several interesting examples in the Science Museum (I).

This escapement or method of checking the fall of the weight and controlling the movement was used by Henry de Vic, a

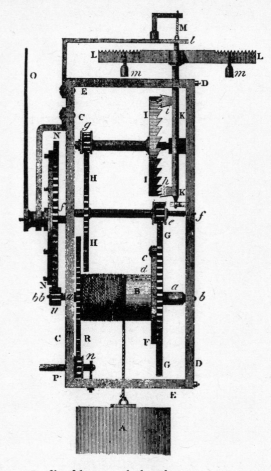

10. Profile of the turret clock with verge escapement and cross-bar or foliot balance made by Henry de Vic for the French king Charles V between 1370 and 1379 (The various parts of this clock are described below)

German clockmaker, with the turret clock he started to make in 1370 and finished in 1379 for Charles V, King of France. A profile of De Vic's clock is shown in (10); and we will, here, add a detailed description of the various parts which are lettered in the illustration.

Like all these ancient clocks, the frame was formed of iron

plates, the front plate *CC* which is angled to form the top and bottom being fastened to the back plate *DD* by nuts. The weight *A* was suspended by a cord wound round the barrel *B* which was prevented from turning backward, when the weight was wound up, by the ratchet *F* and the click or stop *c* pressed into the teeth of the ratchet by a spring *d*. As the massive weight *A* pulled on the cord, it turned the barrel or cylinder *B* and, with it, the great wheel *GG* fixed to the arbor (axle) of the barrel. This great wheel engaged the pinion (small cog wheel) *e* and consequently turned the arbor *ff* and the wheel *HH* at the other end of the arbor; and the wheel *HH*, gearing with the pinion *g* transmitted motion to the crown or, as it is called, escape wheel *II*.

In this way the force exercised by the pull of the weight 'travelled' to the last wheel *II* and so to the vertical spindle or verge *KK* (from verge, a wand or staff) through the action of the wheel on the two small rectangular projections, *i* and *h*, known as pallets, these pallets being attached to the verge *KK* in such a position that they were at almost a right angle. The crown wheel *II* had triangular or ratchet teeth to ensure its moving only in one direction and its progress was checked by the pallets *i* and *h* which, alternately, came against a tooth when it was pushed aside by the pressure of the wheel and the tooth got away or escaped. Thus, when the pallet *i* came against a tooth and the latter had pushed it aside and escaped, the other pallet *h* came against a tooth on the opposite side of the wheel and was similarly disposed of—really a kind of Box and Cox game which continued as long as the clock was in going order. A drawing of the cross bar and verge is shown in (11*a*).

At the same time, the 'stop-go-stop' action of the wheel on the pallets imparted a slight jerk or impulse to the cross-bar or foliot *LL* which, fixed to the verge *KK*, swung to and fro in a semi-rotary movement, the verge being suspended by a light cord to lessen the pressure and so the wear on the pivot (visible in the illustration near the lower letter *K*). The cross-bar *LL* served as a regulator and about half the length of each arm was notched; a small weight being hung in one of the notches on either arm and the clock could be made to go slow or fast by moving these weights *mm* farther from or nearer to the centre as this retarded or increased the speed of the wheel *II*.

Outside the front plate, there was a pinion and a wheel which carried the pointer or hand *O* which indicated the hours on the

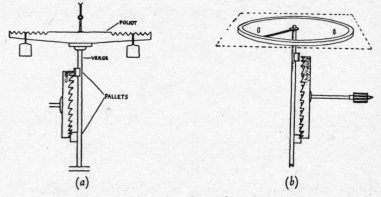

(a)   (b)

11. Details of the verge, the earliest form of recoil escapement with (a) the foliot and adjustable weights and vertical crown wheel and (b) with the later balance wheel

dial. The great wheel *GG* made a complete revolution in an hour and its arbor was extended through the front plate to carry the pinion *u* which engaged the wheel *N* which also made one revolution in an hour. The projecting pins seen in the illustration on the side of wheel *N* were connected with the striking part of De Vic's clock which was similar to, but separate from, the going part.

Some explanation regarding the winding up of the huge weight—it is said to have weighed at least 500 pounds—will be of interest. The winding was done by a key with a handle of the crank type which fitted on the square shown as *P* which was an extension of the arbor of the pinion *n*. To ease the not light task of winding the weight, the wheel *R* was fixed to the barrel *B* and geared with the pinion *n*; this wheel *R* and the barrel were fitted on the arbor so that they could turn separately from the wheel *GG* which was fixed, the connection being made by the ratchet work *F, c, d.* Clocks of a similar character are in the Science

Museum, for example, the Dover Castle clock (I); an early domestic clock with the foliot and crown wheel is shown in (II).

As mentioned, all the early public clocks were massive affairs and entirely too large for domestic use; nor were they by any means reliable time-keepers. Not that this fault was of any great consequence in those days, because people were not so anxious then about the passing minutes as we moderns are. Even so, they did gradually become time-conscious and the more wealthy classes demanded smaller timepieces such as were suitable for carrying when travelling or could even be carried on the person.

Obviously, a clock with a weight was unsuitable, so, material gain and necessity being stimuli to discovery, the early clock-makers sought a more compact and convenient form of driving power. The result was what we now know as the mainspring, the invention of which is ascribed to a German named Peter Hele or Henlein of Nuremberg during the early years of the sixteenth century.

Hele fastened one end of a long steel ribbon to a spindle and by turning the spindle coiled the ribbon tightly round it to drive the movement of a timepiece, thus dispensing with weights. Hele's experiments seem to have been successful, for in 1511 Johannes Cocclaeus speaking of the progress of his period, wrote, 'Ingenious objects are at this time being invented by Peter Hele who is still a young man . . . for he is making small horloges of iron fitted with a number of wheels which, wherever they may be borne, and without a weight show and strike forty hours whether they be carried in the bosom or in the pocket.' Admittedly, this is a somewhat free translation but it expresses the import of the original.

But while these spring-driven timepieces were portable and doubtless pleased their owners, they were far from being accurate time-keepers. A spring confined in a cylindrical drum or barrel has a much greater driving power when it is tightly coiled or fully wound, as we would express it with a clock, for as it uncoils, its outward 'push' becomes weaker and weaker. This can be illustrated by holding a coiled ribbon of steel in the fingers and thumb. It requires more pressure to hold it tightly coiled than it does when the tension of the spring is relaxed.

Always, however, are the drawbacks and weaknesses of man's inventions eventually overcome and corrected. And so it was

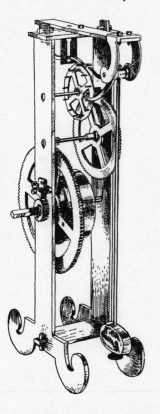

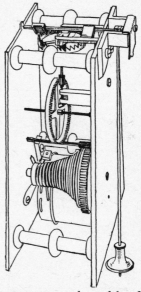

12. (*left*) Reconstructed model of Galileo's escapement and application of the pendulum
Science Museum

13. (*above*) Movement with spring and fusee drive horizontal crown wheel and short pendulum

with Hele's mainspring for clocks. About fifteen years after Cocclaeus had lauded Peter Hele's 'small horloges', Jacob Zech of Prague invented what is known as the fusee (13), though drawings had been made of this ingenious contrivance by Leonardo da Vinci some thirty years before.

Zech's invention, which is still used with certain types of time-pieces, can be seen in many clocks and watches which were made during the eighteenth century and later. It is a spirally grooved tapering cone, known as the fusee, to which a driving wheel is attached and a mainspring coiled in a drum or barrel (13). A catgut line is fastened at one end to the fusee and at the other to the barrel; the catgut was later replaced by a tiny chain with links similar to those of a bicycle chain and those used in watches are almost too small to see with the naked eye; in some clocks a cabled wire was used.

Unlike later spring-driven movements with which the spring itself is wound, the fusee is turned by a key; this draws the catgut line or chain on to the spiral grooves of the fusee and tightly coils the spring inside the barrel. In order that the line or chain shall not be given unnecessary strain when the fusee has been turned sufficiently to wind it fully, a small stop is so fitted that it automatically prevents the fusee being turned.

After being fully wound, the mainspring straining to uncoil itself causes the barrel to turn in the reverse direction and so pulls the catgut or chain from the fusee and winds it round the barrel, starting the pull from the small end of the tapering cone. As it begins to pull, the power of the mainspring which is wound fully is much stronger than it will become as it unwinds. As it unwinds, it loses more and more of its power, but this is compensated by the increasing circumference of the fusee as the line is drawn on to the barrel—in technical language the gradual increase in the size of the fusee maintains the equipollence, i.e. the equality in the pulling power of the mainspring.

But even with this improvement, no clock that would record the passing hours accurately was known until some few years after the introduction of the pendulum more than a century later. When this important addition was first adopted is uncertain, but Galileo, the Italian astronomer (1564–1642) is generally credited with its invention.

It is told that while watching a lamp swinging in the cathedral of Pisa, in about 1590, he noticed that whether the swings were long or short, the time of each swing was apparently identical. He began to experiment with a view to proving this phenomenon and the result was he decided that a pendulum was isochronal—in plainer English, it always swung back and forth in the same period of time irrespective of the extent of the swing. The pendulum was first used for timing astronomical observations, but it was then started by hand and kept swinging by a gentle push at intervals and the number of the swings counted by someone who watched it closely.

Galileo later conceived a method by which the pendulum could be applied to a simple mechanism with a rude type of escapement; but while Galileo and his son Vicenzio are known to have devoted their attention to the problem, and to have made drawings of a pendulum clock, there is some doubt as to whether they succeeded in making a clock controlled by a pendulum. There is, however, a reconstruction of a working model of Galileo's escapement at the Science Museum, though this does not have the weight by which it was driven in the original design (12).

Doubt exists as to when satisfactory pendulum clocks were first made but it is generally conceded that it was in 1657 when a Dutch astronomer, Christian Huygens, produced a pendulum clock. He also determined that the time occupied by the swing was not entirely unaffected by its length or arc as Galileo had decided. Huygens remedied this, however, by suspending the pendulum by two cords between two curved pieces of flexible steel, known as cycloidal cheeks; later the cords were replaced by a thin piece of steel spring and the rod of the pendulum was fitted with a 'crutch'. This crutch which can be seen with any grandfather or later bracket clock (15), is at right angles with a short rod fixed to the arbor (axle) carrying the escape—its purpose is explained fully in Chapter Eight.

Huygens' clock which is illustrated (14) had several ingenious features. The main driving weight P was suspended by a pulley d on a cord with the ends joined. This endless cord passed over the pulley A in Figure 14b (this is D in 14), which was on the arbor of the great or first wheel CC, and under the pulley f carrying the counter weight p. It then passed up and over the ratchet pulley H which turned on a stud fastened to the inside of the back plate. When the cord m was pulled down to raise the main weight, that is to wind the clock, the ratchet wheel H and its click came into play and prevented the weight P from falling and both the pulleys

H and *A* had steel points in the groove to stop the cord from slipping. By this contrivance, the power was maintained while the clock was being wound up.

As the weight turned the pulley *D* (this is *A* in 14*b*) and the first wheel *CC* on the same arbor, the wheel engaged the pinion *E* and so put in motion the wheel *F*. This wheel, through the pinion *G* above it, carried the drive to *H*, known as the contrate wheel, which engaging the horizontal pinion *I* put the crown wheel *K* in motion. The crown wheel had triangular teeth to ensure its going only in one direction, as explained with the De Vic clock, and was checked by the two pallets *LL* on the horizontal verge *LM*, part of which (*M*) extended beyond the frame and carried a crutch with a loop through which the pendulum rod passed, the rod and its large bob *X* being suspended by two strong threads between cycloidal cheeks *T*—the cheeks and method of suspending the pendulum are shown more clearly in the small illustration (14*a*).

Earlier in this chapter, we referred to the action of the crown wheel on the pallets imparting an impulse to the cross-bar balance. This action had the same effect on the pendulum of Huygens' clock. As the teeth of the crown wheel *K* alternately lifted the pallets in opposite directions and escaped, it naturally caused the horizontal verge *LM* to vibrate; and as the verge was fixed at *M* to the crutch *S*, the latter must also vibrate and so give a push to the swing of the pendulum.

Between the dial *gg* and the front plate there were other wheels connected with the hands. The arbor of the first wheel *CC* continued through the front plate and the dial and this arbor carried the socket of the wheel *a*, the minute hand being put on at *e*. The wheel *a* engaged the wheel *b* which had the same number of teeth while the pinion on the arbor of *b* engaged the wheel *d*; the socket or pipe of this last wheel fitted over that of *a* and carried the hour hand. A small dial *ff* was marked to show the seconds which were indicated by a pointer fitted to the end of the arbor of wheel *H*.

Though after the adoption of the pendulum (to the verge escapement) there was some improvement in the time-keeping

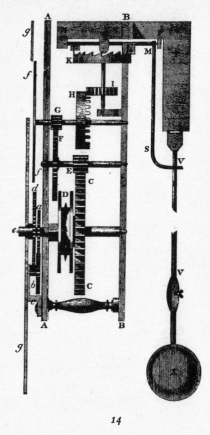

14a

14

14. Pendulum clock with verge escapement constructed by Huygens in 1657

14a. Cycloidal cheeks, crutch and
method of hanging the pendulum

14b

14b. Weights with endless cord for maintaining the power when winding
(The various parts of this clock are described in detail on pp. 27, 28)

qualities of clocks, it was not until the invention of the 'anchor' escapement that any real accuracy was achieved. Furthermore, the arc or swing of the pendulum was greatly reduced by the use of this device which made it possible to enclose a pendulum clock movement in a small case.

This important invention is generally credited to Dr. Robert Hooke who made a model for the reconstruction of the City of London after the great fire in 1666 and who was described by John Aubrey in his *Minutes of Lives* as of 'prodigious inventive head'. The escapement derives its name 'anchor' from its being shaped like the curved arms and each end having a tooth-like shape projecting inward which somewhat resembles the flukes of an anchor (15). The technical name of these projecting 'teeth' is pallet (from *pala*, a spade).

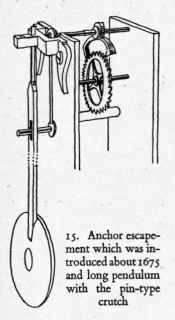

15. Anchor escapement which was introduced about 1675 and long pendulum with the pin-type crutch

As the pendulum swings, the curved bar of the anchor rocks in a see-saw movement and, as one side comes down, the pallet on that side comes into contact with a tooth of the escape wheel which is set vertically immediately below; then as the pendulum continues its swing in the same direction the pallet slides down toward the base of the tooth. When the pendulum swings in the other direction, it lifts the anchor arm and consequently the tooth escapes, and the pallet on the other arm comes down and repeats the action on the opposite side of the escape wheel. But, because each pallet slides well down the side of each tooth, it does not escape before causing the pendulum to recoil or, as it were, be stopped with a slight jerk and this gives the pendulum an impulse for its 'swing back'. This recoil can be noticed in the slight shiver of the second hand of a grandfather clock.

In developing this escapement, Hooke made possible the use of the long pendulum which he had for long contended would ensure better timekeeping, as it did after it was adopted. Until the introduction of the anchor escapement, the only pendulum used was the short kind with a small bob (13); this was fitted to the verge escapement which was modified by placing the escape wheel and verge horizontally and fitting the short pendulum to the end. As explained earlier, two pallets were fixed to the verge which, being at right angles with the pendulum, oscillated with the swing and so the pallets alternately came against a tooth in the escape wheel, and checked the pull of the weight which was the driving power.

More will be said in later chapters of both the short and the long pendulum and the change brought about with domestic clocks as a result of the introduction of the latter.

SECTION 3

Timepieces for Modern Rooms

CHAPTER SIX

LANTERN CLOCKS

SMALL CLOCKS SUITABLE for use in a house were known earlier in Europe, but it seems improbable that any were made in this country before the later years of the sixteenth century. The first movements were a series of stout iron wheels in a rectangular iron frame (II) driven by weights, with the verge escapement and, possibly, the foliot balance, i.e. the oscillating cross-bar with a weight at each end shown in (11*a*); there is little evidence, however, that the foliot was used by English clockmakers.

These clocks are variously known as 'bedpost', 'birdcage', 'lantern', and for some unknown reason are often referred to as 'Cromwellian'; they are, however, more generally called lantern clocks. And though we now speak of a clock in a wood case intended to be placed on a mantel or a table as a bracket clock, strictly speaking this should apply to lantern clocks, because the latter had to be placed on a bracket to allow for the fall of the cords and weights, the cords passing through holes cut in the bracket. All these lantern clocks had movements which ran for thirty hours and they were wound by pulling the opposite end of the cords and raising the weights.

There is an interesting sixteenth-century example at the Science Museum (II). This has the original verge escapement and foliot with two quite sturdy weights and a large gong supported by four strips of iron surmounted by a finial. The sides and back are open, but the front has a moulded arched plate to which an hour ring with a quite elaborate pierced centre is applied and like almost all lantern clocks, it has only one hand or pointer; we are able to illustrate a rare example of one with a minute hand in (III).

Within a few years of their becoming popular with the more wealthy, the movements were enclosed in a case of brass and almost at the same time brass replaced iron for the various wheels. The case was formed by a brass pillar at each corner linking the

16. Brass lantern clock, the first type of timepiece for domestic use

17. Various styles of ornaments, known as frets, which were used with the brass lantern clocks in the seventeenth, eighteenth and early nineteenth centuries

top and bottom, a plate at the back, a similar plate with a silvered hour ring engraved with the numerals at the front, while each of the sides was enclosed by a brass door (16). Any fitted with the short pendulum placed between the going and the striking train, as it was occasionally, had a slot cut in each of the doors; this was necessary because the swing of the pendulum being wider than the clock, the slots allowed the disc to 'bob out and in'.

Considerable decoration was added to lantern clocks by the use of engraving and what are known as frets. The brass plates were finely engraved, particularly that part of the front within the hour ring (16); and in view of the variation of the ornamental work on the doors, it might seem that these were often engraved to a design selected by the person for whom the clock was made.

But the most noticeable ornaments with lantern clocks are the so-called 'frets' fitted at the top of the front and sides, presumably to conceal the space between the top of the case and the bell. These frets with an original clock may be an indication, though not an infallible one, of the approximate period at which it was made. Frets in the form of a shield with mantling were used with some of the earliest examples; others of the first half of the seventeenth century were intricate designs of scrollings some of which embodied the fleur-de-lys, while others finish in the centre in the form of two monsters' heads. In other instances, a large vase would form the centre of a series of scrollings, sometimes surmounted by a bird (17).

In the fret with the monsters' heads, it is possible to see an early form of the crossed dolphin design which was adopted fairly generally and became popular after about 1640 and which remained the favourite until lantern clocks went out of fashion. A rarer, later design was a shield surmounted by a crown with supporters intended for the lion and the unicorn. Again, the frets with clocks by provincial makers vary to some extent according to the district and some of the quite late ones are often crudely finished; for lantern clocks were made in country districts until the last century, at which time the pride of craftsmanship was tending to decline.

Some larger lantern clocks were made before the end of the

seventeenth century, and several examples of these have survived. Most of them, however, had cases about 3 to 5 inches high with the addition of the gong and its finial. During the late seventeenth and early eighteenth centuries, the diameter of the dial was increased without any proportionate increase in the size of the case with the result that the dial would project noticeably on each side and detract from the otherwise good proportions.

When these first domestic or chamber clocks, as they are also referred to, came into use, they were by no means cheap; consequently, it was not usual in those days to have a timepiece in different parts of the house. This explains the large bell which was always fitted to the top of lantern clocks, one of which would be placed in some central position, such as the hall, from which the striking of hours would be heard in other parts of the house. This tradition we continue to the present day in the custom of putting the family grandfather clock in the hall, from which position its sonorous bell can be heard downstairs and upstairs.

Lantern clocks were also fitted with an alarum and any with this addition may be identified by their having a small dial behind the hand with the hour numbers in arabic figures (18a), though roman were used in some instances. Others both struck the hours and chimed the quarters on a series of smaller bells placed below the large one and a few are known which send forth more or less musical tunes.

Details of the mechanism of an early clock with an alarum are shown in (18). The going part of this, i.e. between the plates DC, is similar to that of Huygens' clock described in the preceding chapter. But instead of the pendulum, the clock (18) had a vertical balance M which vibrated to and fro and was impelled by the action of the wheel L on the pallets l and m, which, alternately, dropped in and were lifted out from a tooth of the crown wheel L as it escaped, also, the method of suspending the weights F and R and the counter weights G and S was less complicated than that adopted by Huygens.

There is a noticeable simplicity, too, with the alarum mechanism which is in the back frame ON. The cord by which the weight and counter weight were suspended passed over the pulley Q in a similar way to that of the going part; and the pulley made a kind of ratchet and click with the wheel P when the counter weight was pulled down to wind up the weight R. This wheel P with the pallets o and n was the escapement, the pallets being on the vertical verge which continued upwards to the short angled arm pp, qq which carried the alarum hammer x; this hammer was cylindrical with hemispherical ends which struck alternately on the inside edges of the bell (not shown in the illustration).

On the outside of the wheel P there was a pin (visible in the diagram) which came against the small projection p and stopped the alarum after the weight was wound up. The dial of the alarum and a counter spring s were on a socket fitted over the socket of the hour wheel f and at the time set on the dial (A in the figure), a pin lifted the arm r of the contrivance pqr, known as a detent; this raised the small projection at p, released the wheel P which at once began to turn and the hammer x started to hit the bell right lustily and arouse the sleeper and all nearby.

We have mentioned earlier that the lantern clock was actually the original bracket clock. This would seem obvious from the fact that the cases were almost invariably raised on feet, from the time of their first appearance, when both the case and the wheels of the movement were made of iron (II). But it is evident, too, that some were intended to be fastened to a wall without a bracket, because a fair number are known which are fitted with what are called a stirrup and spurs. The stirrup was a large metal loop fixed to the top of the case at the back and the spurs, a long spike on each of the back legs; the stirrup was fastened to the wall, by a staple or a hook and the spurs driven firmly into the wall, the latter ensuring support to the clock and weights and the stirrup preventing it from pulling forward at the top.

While the foliot (cross-bar with weights) was used, it was superseded within a short time by the balance wheel control. This wheel was horizontal and had a semi-rotary or forward and backward movement. At each swing, the wheel came against a stud, which both restricted the arc and caused the wheel to rebound and swing in reverse when it came against a stud on the

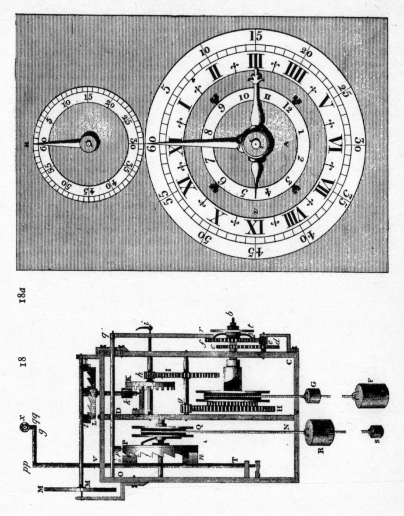

18

18*a*

18. Profile of a weight-driven clock with vertical balance and alarum

(The mechanism of the alarum part is described on pp. 35, 36)

18a. Dials of the clock illustrated in fig. 18. The dial *A* is that of the alarum

opposite side. As the balance wheel made its to and fro movement, it caused the vertical spindle or verge to which it was fixed
to turn in a similar way and the pallets on the verge then alternately engaged and released the escape wheel. This device in no
way improved the time-keeping qualities of the clocks, however,
because of the lack of any means of regulating the wheel other
than by increasing or decreasing the size of the driving weight.

It is not suggested that this form of control was retained,
because there is little doubt that after the pendulum was adopted,
in about 1660, more and more of the balance escapements were
converted and fitted with a short pendulum as described in
Chapter Five. Where this conversion has been made with an
early clock—as it was to very many for the purpose of ensuring
more accurate time-keeping—there are various indications of its
once having had a balance wheel. Toward the end of the
seventeenth century the traditional cords and weights began to
give place to the coiled spring in a barrel and the fusee wound by
a key (see Chapter Five) which needing no space below allowed
a clock to be placed on a shelf or a table; and this was soon
followed by other improvements pointing the way to the splendid
timepieces which brought to the British clock and watchmakers
pre-eminence throughout the world.

With the adoption of the spring drive, clocks, as it were, came
to the parting of the ways. The spring-driven lantern movement
was enclosed in a wooden hood or case instead of the brass case
to become what we now call the bracket clock; while the weight-
driven lantern movement, also enclosed in a hood with the weights
exposed below, became the popular hanging wall clock and, with
the hood and a cupboard-like case to conceal the weights, gave
us the first long case or as it is generally called, the grandfather
clock.

As might be expected, very few of these 'ancient' grandfather
clocks exist to-day and they differ markedly from those which are
generally familiar to us moderns. Most of them are about 6 feet
high with a small dial and hood and, below, a narrow case similar
to a narrow cupboard such as is sometimes built into a small recess
at the side of a fireplace in old houses—and the doors of the clock

cases are usually panelled in the same
style as the cupboards (19). But if on
examination they differ from their
descendants, little difference is apparent
in the general appearance of the dial. It
is admittedly smaller, but by the time
the wood case made its appearance, the
minute hand had been adopted and the
earlier single pointer virtually discarded.

While they were eventually superseded
in fashionable circles of the later
eighteenth century by the clocks with
wood cases, brass lantern clocks continued to be made for some years afterwards, particularly by provincial clockmakers. Some of these late country-
made clocks have the arch dial and in
country homes and inns you may
occasionally come upon one fitted in a
hood-like case of wood on a bracket with
the weights and pendulum exposed.

It might, perhaps, be well to refer to
the widely held idea that all lantern
clocks in brass are 'antique', in the real
sense of this much misused adjective.
Even if an example did once belong to a
favourite great-aunt of the present owner,
it does not denote that the clock is earlier
than the nineteenth century; yet we have
often heard a modern copy referred to as
'Cromwellian' and have realized that the
owner is under the impression it was made
during England's totalitarian régime.

In many instances, these later clocks are
excellent modern reproductions and if
they are not genuine antiques, they can
be and are more or less skilfully 'antiqued'

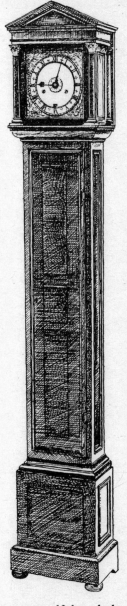

19. Grandfather clock.
By Joseph Knibb, c. 1680

by one of the several processes employed for this purpose. Perhaps it may not be what you have imagined, yet, if one of the better made copies, it, at least, records the hours and minutes more accurately than one of its seventeenth-century forbears with the verge and balance wheel or even with the little 'tick-tack' pendulum.

In fact, many who prefer service to sentiment and who have come into possession of an old lantern clock, have had the original movement replaced by a more reliable modern one. The purpose of a clock is to 'tell the time' and whatever its age one that does not work, while ornamental, can be irritating. Few things are more provoking than to be continually looking at a clock whose hands never move.

CHAPTER SEVEN

SMALLER PORTABLE TIMEPIECES

ANY CLOCK OF A size suitable for carrying must obviously be small, but the qualifying 'smaller' in the heading is added as this chapter deals with the portable timepieces made long before those we now call bracket clocks which also belong to the category of 'portable', as a stout handle at the top of the case indicates.

After Peter Hele of Nuremberg invented the coiled spring (see Chapter Five) and produced 'small horloges', there was an immediate demand for portable timepieces. It was some considerable time, however, before any were made that could be 'carried in the bosom or in the pocket' as Cocclaeus described those produced by Hele; but his invention and, more particularly, the introduction of the fusee and spring by Jacob Zech did result in the appearance of small clocks that could be placed on the table and others that could be carried when travelling. And there are an appreciable number of others which have been preserved that are very similar to, though more elaborate and much larger than the later pocket watches—actually they are small clocks.

We are reproducing an illustration (20) from a work by the famous horologist, Ferdinand Berthoud, as it gives an unusually clear picture of a spring-driven movement with a balance and verge escapement for a small portable clock.

One end of the spring OP (shown here without the barrel) was hooked to the lower part of the arbor of the first or great wheel N and the other end to the barrel; the ratchet X with its click m and spring n being fixed to the arbor of the wheel N in such a way that, in winding the spring, the arbor and ratchet turned independently from the wheel.

This first wheel N engaged the pinion a and thus set in motion the second wheel M which is lower on the same arbor as the pinion and the second wheel, engaging the pinion b turned the third wheel L which, through the pinion c, transmitted the drive to the horizontal wheel K, known as the contrate wheel. This contrate wheel, by the pinion d carried the drive to the crown wheel C which, as its teeth escaped the pallets pp on the verge, gave an impulse to the balance A which had an alternating or semi-rotary movement—that is, it swung to and fro in the arc of a circle.

From this illustration, there is no difficulty in following the 'journey' of the outward push of the spring OP which, when wound up, set all the wheels in motion; the force of its push being controlled by the ratchet work and the motion of the wheels by the interference of the pallets pp with the teeth of the crown or escape wheel C.

Between the dial and the front plate, there are two wheels and two pinions which 'guide' the hands. Their movement comes direct from the first wheel N through the pinion a which turns the arbor of the second wheel M and, consequently, the pinion Q on the extended arbor, the socket of which goes beyond the dial to the square for the minute hand. The pinion Q engages the minute wheel T while the pinion g on the arbor of the minute wheel, acts upon the hour wheel V which has a hollow socket or pipe and carries the hour hand.

As the use of a spring to drive a clock was first adopted by a German clockmaker, it was natural that the first examples of portable timepieces should have originated in that country; and there is evidence to suggest they were made there as early as about 1505. Toward the end of that century, they were being produced in Holland and France; and while some were produced later in this country, judging from the very few early surviving examples the number made by English clockmakers must have been quite small.

One of the earliest known English portable clocks is in the British Museum. It was made by Bartholomew Newsam who is believed to have been born in Yorkshire and who later established himself in the Strand near Somerset House early in the reign of Queen Elizabeth and, in 1583, was appointed clockmaker to the Queen.

Its form and treatment is shown in the illustration (63). The case is of engraved and gilded brass about 4 inches high and $2\frac{1}{2}$ inches square, the pierced dome and finial increasing the height to

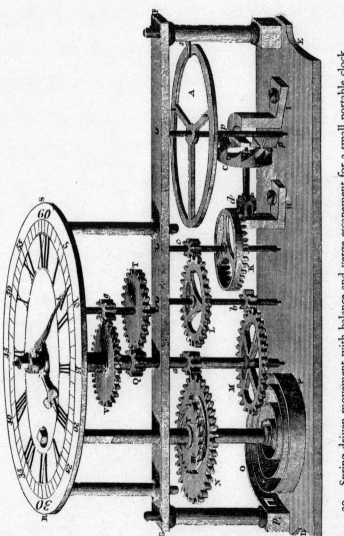

20. Spring-driven movement with balance and verge escapement for a small portable clock

slightly over 6 inches. It has a striking train and the bell is placed under the dome at the top, the ornamental piercings of which are to allow the sound of the bell to be heard more clearly. All the wheels are of iron or steel, as was customary before the use of brass, and both the going and striking trains have a fusee connected by catgut to a barrel containing the spring and it has the verge escapement.

It is wound by a key which fits two winding holes in the bottom of the case, and a quaint little arched window at each side allows a sight of the fusees to ascertain when they need rewinding. This rare clock has another interesting feature: The engraved centre that is within the hour circle, instead of being an integral part of the case is recessed slightly and fastened to the movement; the purpose of this is to allow the complete movement with the hand and dial centre to be taken out of the case after first detaching the bottom.

Earlier German spring-driven clocks with cases similar to that by Newsam have been preserved in different museums and private collections. All of these, however, are of a very much more ornamental character and with many there is an obvious architectural influence, which is apparent in the magnificent cases formed like a high tower with classic columns and caps as corner posts supporting the upper structure.

Spring-driven small portable clocks by early English clockmakers are known, but examples are few and far between. They have a horizontal dial on a cylindrical or square case copied from the continental models and are about 3 inches high, so would serve equally well on a table or, if protected in a case, were suitable for carrying when travelling. The more simple type have a low drum-shaped case sometimes raised on feet with a wide hour ring applied to the rim of the top and are decorated with embossed or engraved designs (V). There is a similar elaboration with the square table clocks (64), the case being rather like a small box with an engraved hour ring and single hand on the top.

Many of the surviving specimens of these small table clocks have a high pierced dome with a small dial engraved with the hours and a hand on top of the dome. The highly ornamental

character of some of these clocks can be illustrated by an example
in the Victoria and Albert Museum.   This (VI) is one of the few
known English clocks of this kind; it was made by David Ramsay
who had a shop near Temple Bar during the reign of James I.
The excellent workmanship of the case, however, permits the
assumption that while Ramsay made the movement, the case
was the work of a skilled continental artist-craftsman.

In fact the ornamental treatment of the case would suggest it
was the work of a French craftsman.   It is supported on four lion
feet and has a caryatid at each corner, each of the four sides being
decorated with an applied oval panel engraved with figures
flanked on each side by a winged figure amid intricate foliated
scroll work.   The pierced design of the domed top is equally
elaborate and French in character.   And there are some English
cylindrical table clocks of this type with both the domed top and
the entire case pierced.

To-day, the word 'watch' is firmly established as denoting a
small timepiece that may be carried in the pocket or worn on the
wrist, while a clock refers to one which should not normally be
moved from one place to another.   Which recalls an amusing
incident we enjoyed in Pall Mall some years ago: A porter had
been sent to collect a grandfather clock from a nearby auction
room; apparently he didn't realize the size for he had no barrow
and carried it away in his arms.   As he passed along the street, a
mischievous but bright lad called to him, 'Siy whoi doncher buy
yerself a wrist watch?'

Formerly the words 'clock' and 'watch' were applied in-
determinately to any time-teller—'watch' was even used to denote
a candle marked in divisions, each of which would be consumed
by the lighted wick in a certain period of time.   And William
Derham (1657-1735) one-time vicar of Wargrave and a canon
of Windsor, in the several editions of his scientific work on
different types of timekeepers, *The Artificial Clock-Maker*,
published first in 1696, consistently restricts 'clock' to the striking
mechanism and refers to a weight-driven timepiece as a 'watch'.

Though many of the first portable timepieces of the clock-
watch type were fitted in circular cases with a bow or ring by

which they might be carried, they have no other resemblance to what we know as a watch. Actually, a century passed after the invention of the spring by Peter Hele and the appearance of spring-driven portable clocks before timekeepers, small enough to carry in the pocket or wear suspended from a chain round the neck, were made in any appreciable numbers.

What the clock-watches lacked as timekeepers was, perhaps, compensated to their aristocratic owners by the magnificence of the cases. These were, to all intents, a cylindrical box with a hinged cover rather like the watches we speak of as 'hunter'; but, in place of being plain metal, the covers were beautifully chased and engraved and had a small opening over each hour numeral so that the position of the pointer was visible to tell the time. Glass for covering a clock dial was adopted on the Continent in the late sixteenth century but was not generally used until some fifty years later.

As a rule, they were fitted with a bell which struck the hours, for which reason the back of the case was perforated by cutting away the background of the design to allow the sound of the bell to be heard more distinctly. If the possibility of becoming the owner of one of these interesting old timepieces is remote, and if few by English clockmakers are known, there are a number of splendid specimens in the British and the Victoria and Albert museums, including one in a crystal case by Edward East who had a shop in Pall Mall and was clockmaker to Charles I.

East is said to have made a large clock-watch for Charles I which was kept at the side of the king's bed. This timepiece, which had an alarum, was in a circular silver case with the back pierced and chased with a large central rose blossom surrounded by sprays of English flowers; the rim of the front being similarly decorated and the centre of the dial within the hour-ring painted with a rural scene. It is traditionally supposed to have been given by Charles I to Sir Thomas Herbert on the day the king was executed.

In the later years of the seventeenth century, large clock-watches for travelling were introduced and these remained popular (and expensive) until the old horse-drawn coach gave place to the railway. Most of the known 'coach-clocks', as they are called, are of continental origin, but some examples by English clockmakers have survived. These were no timepieces to be carried in the fob-pocket; they measured from three to seven inches in diameter and were proportionately thick and heavy. The earlier ones had a bell which struck the hour and usually an alarum. Later, however, the alarum was replaced by a repeating action which, by pulling a string on the outside of the case, repeated the number of strokes struck previously on the hour-bell. The cases, usually of silver, were elaborately chased and pierced and many were furnished with an additional outer case which would be covered with leather to protect the clock when travelling.

If these massive 'watches' have now to be counted among the very rare rarities, it is still possible to obtain one of those later attractive portable timepieces generally referred to as 'sedan chair clocks' or, to give them another earlier name, 'post-chaise clocks'; moreover, they are better timekeepers than the older 'travelling' clocks. They were made during the eighteenth and early nineteenth centuries and have clearly legible dials, either silvered or enamel, fitted in polished wood frames.

Incidentally, the sedan-chair was in general use as a means of transport during the eighteenth century, but it had been introduced to this country from the Continent in the time of Charles I. In certain health-resorts where there are mineral-water baths, it was used until fairly recent times to convey a patient from his house to the baths; and though no longer a form of transport, one of these comfortable 'carriages' is yet to be seen in the hall of some clubs and other semi-public buildings.

Its horse-drawn counterparts were a light carriage with a folding hood, known as a 'calash' and the post-chaise which was used for fast travelling. The post-chaise was a four-wheeled closed carriage usually drawn by four horses with the driver riding postillion; that is on the near side leading horse or, if only two horses, on the near side one of the pair.

There is little evidence that English seventeenth-century makers essayed those more ambitious clocks or the horological curiosities

made in Germany and elsewhere, of which examples are preserved in private and public collections. We have already referred
to the popularity in Germany of clock cases in the form of towers,
some of which were upward of 2 feet high often with several
dials showing, respectively, the date, the day of the week, phases
of the moon and other astronomical data; and such clocks usually
sounded the hour and the quarter hours, which would obviously
call for more than ordinary knowledge and skill in making the
necessarily involved mechanism.

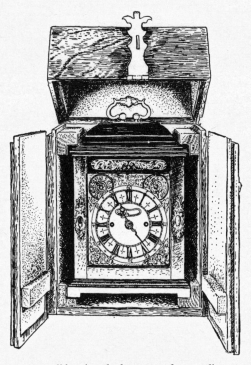

21. Small bracket clock in a case for travelling. It
has a pendulum aperture in the dial and two
subsidiary dials, one for regulating and the other
for controlling the striking. It has a pull-repeat
movement by Thomas Tompion and Edward
Banger, c. 1700

CHAPTER EIGHT

BRACKET CLOCKS

FOLLOWING THE RULE observed by St. Ambrose as to his behaviour in Milan and in Rome, we conform to the accepted custom in applying the term 'bracket clock' to those much admired time-pieces which, to-day, are to be seen usually on a mantel. If, however, we were submissive to purism, this chapter head would be 'Portable Mantel and Table Clocks' because they were intended to be carried from room to room for which reason a stout handle was fixed above the case—later cases have a handle on each side.

22. Engraved back plate of a bracket clock with ornamental cock concealing the pendulum suspension

That they were commonly placed on a table is confirmed by a feature found with all the finer bracket clocks and one often overlooked, i.e. the finely engraved designs on the brass back-plate of the movement (22) and the fact that the back door is glazed.

Obviously, this indicates that the back of the clock was intended to be seen as it would be when on a table. Grandfather clocks which were essentially wall pieces, and were not infrequently fastened to a wall, have a similar brass plate, but this is invariably plain.

It is noticeable, too, that as clocks were produced in larger quantities and therefore became cheaper during the early nineteenth century, the engraving of the back plates of bracket clocks was discontinued and the back door no longer fitted with glass. Not that these later clocks are any less reliable as timekeepers, but they lack those signs of the craftsman's pride in his handiwork which raise it to a work of art; and if many of us moderns do not immediately notice these 'little touches', we unconsciously miss them if they are absent.

Another indication that the back of earlier bracket clocks was exposed to view is an ornament known as a 'cock' which was fixed to the back-plate to conceal the suspension of the pendulum (22). These elaborate ornaments are relatively large and those of the earlier bracket clocks are excellent examples of tooled and engraved work.

From what has been said of the development of the lantern clock in a preceding chapter, it will be seen that it was the immediate ancestor of those with movements fitted in wooden cases, we speak of as bracket clocks. The latter made their appearance during the second half of the seventeenth century and were popular before the grandfather became fashionable. The first examples were plain rather squat box-like cases with a portico (23) or flat top. It was not long, however, before more advanced cases were made and enriched with metal mounts; more will be said later in this chapter of the several styles of cases indicative of the period at which a clock was made.

Like the later spring-driven lantern clocks, the early bracket clocks in wood cases had the verge escapement, the fusee and spring drive and the short pendulum with the small bob (13). And though the anchor escapement was introduced about 1675 and this allowed a longer pendulum with a shorter arc of swing, it does not seem that these improvements were generally adopted with bracket clocks until about the middle of Queen Anne's reign; but once the advantages of the anchor escapement and long pendulum were recognized, many of the clocks with the verge were later converted.

Radical changes were also made with the pendulum. With

23. Early bracket clock with lunar disc in ebony case with portico top and columns with gilt metal caps, c. 1690

the first bracket clocks, the pendulum was fastened to the horizontal verge and operated as described with the later lantern clocks. But after the adoption of the anchor escapement, and the larger and heavier disc or bob, the pendulum was suspended by a short piece of flexible steel ribbon (called the suspension spring) from the 'jaws' of the 'cock'—in everyday language, the slit in the protruding bracket fixed to the top of the back plate.

Obviously, a pendulum hanging from a piece of spring in this way has no connection with the movement of a clock. The connection is made by what is known as a 'crutch'. This is a light steel rod with an arm in the form of a pin, a loop or a fork set at a right angle with the lower end of the rod, the other end being fixed to the arbor (axle) of the anchor, technically called the pallet arbor (15). When the crutch is the pin type, the pin passes through a slot in a flat pendulum rod; otherwise the latter passes through the loop or rides in the fork. As the pendulum swings, it carries with it the crutch, lifting first one pallet and then the other of the anchor from the escape wheel which, in turn, counts off the seconds and minutes.

But though the long pendulum with the heavy disc and anchor escapement was adopted to weight-driven clocks by the foremost makers during the last quarter of the seventeenth century, it does not seem to have been used with spring-driven clocks until some years later; and even after that time, clocks by some makers were still fitted with the short pendulum and verge. This is explained by the fact that as bracket clocks were formerly carried from one room to another, the short pendulum and verge was less likely to be affected by any consequent jolting than the heavy disc and anchor; it was, in fact, customary when moving a clock with the latter escapement to lift the pendulum from the jaws and some clocks were fitted with a device for locking the pendulum to prevent its vibrating when being carried.

Like their predecessor, the lantern clock, bracket clocks from their first appearance were almost invariably fitted with a striking train which sounded the hours. Some also chimed the quarter-hours and some have a repeating mechanism when they may be identified by a small string or cord hanging from the side of the case, though this was, in rare instances, placed under the case. When this string is pulled, the clock will strike the last quarter followed by the number of strokes corresponding to the last hour (24).

Bracket clocks with mechanism which played various tunes were made by the more expert clockmakers and these enjoyed considerable popularity during the eighteenth century among those who could afford such luxuries. These musical clocks were an adaptation of the old musical box which consisted of flat steel springs in the form of a comb vibrated by pins on a brass cylinder and sent forth sounds of a not always tuneful character. These erstwhile 'family instruments' were relatively common about a century ago and examples are still available to those interested in curiosities. Incidentally, it is often suggested it was a nineteenth-century invention, but the musical box of that period is, to all intents, a copy of one known several centuries before.

For their musical clocks, the clockmakers borrowed the

24. Walnut basket-top case with repeating movement operated by a cord at the side. Early type of corner ornaments, *c.* 1700

cylinder with the pins and applied it to the mechanism of the timepiece fitted with a series of, usually, twelve bells each with a different tone. At certain times, either at the hour or at 12, 3, 6 and 9, the cylinder revolves bringing various pins against the tail of one of the hammers, causing it to lift and fall on its own particular bell; in this way a sequence of strokes on the different

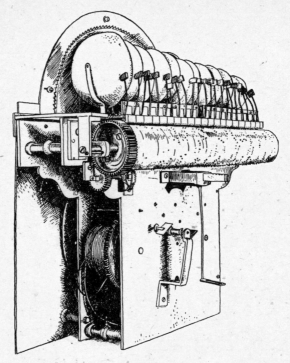

25. Details of a musical clock movement with twelve
bells and cylinder with pins that operate the hammers.
Late eighteenth century

bells formed a tune in a similar way to, but usually more har-
monious than the pins pushing against the steel springs of the old
musical box (25).

Musical clocks that play at longer intervals, namely, every three
hours, usually repeat the tune twice or possibly three times. And
realizing that the same air is apt to become monotonous, the
clockmakers developed a method by which the cylinder might
be moved and the tune changed; more ambitious clocks have
additional interchangeable cylinders, each playing a number of
different tunes and examples are known having two hammers
which strike the same bell when the music is prestissimo.

Some of the musical bracket clocks have the titles of the various
tunes engraved in the arch of the dial, though few of the airs are

familiar to the present generation. The clock shown in the frontispiece was made by George Graham (1673–1751), one of England's most celebrated clockmakers. It plays twelve tunes, and the engraved titles include *Lt. Hoods Delight; Astleys Hornpipe; Forest Hunt; Richmonds Minuet; Mirth & Glee; Robinson Crusoe* and others long since forgotten. A pointer connected with the musical mechanism is fixed above the hour ring and by moving this to the desired title on the arch, the clock plays the tune indicated. A cheery moon-face shows the phases of the moon in the arch and there is a small dial on each side marked 'Strike—Not Strike' and 'Chime—Not Chime' each with a small pointer, controlling, respectively, the striking and the music.

As a general rule, the name of the man who made the movement of a fine clock is engraved on the dial or back plate, but the names of the men who designed and made the cases are forgotten. Yet, from the time when the anchor escapement allowed for a shorter arc or swing of the pendulum and movements were enclosed in wooden cases, the latter progressed to a degree of restrained beauty which distinguishes the work of the English eighteenth-century case makers from that of all other countries, though some of the designs were copied successfully by American makers of clock cases.

As mentioned earlier, portable clocks in wooden cases of the type we know as bracket clocks were introduced during the later seventeenth century. The first were similar to a smaller edition of the hood of a grandfather clock, i.e. simple box-like affairs with a flat top, a square glazed door in the front and back, and usually a glass panel at each side. Another early case, often of ebony, was of an architectural character, with a portico top and columns on each side in front; and occasionally the capitals and bases of these columns were of cast and finely tooled brass (23).

One of the portico style came to the writer's notice when the Wetherfield clocks were dispersed. This famous collection which consisted of more than two hundred clocks was assembled over a period of some forty years by Mr. David Wetherfield. After his death, the whole collection was scheduled to be sold at auction in 1928, but, before the date of the sale, it was purchased privately, part of it being acquired by a London dealer and the remainder by Arthur S. Vernay of New York. The latter had a descriptive catalogue prepared of the hundred odd clocks he acquired and the writer was fortunate in being associated with this; fortunate, because it allowed an opportunity to examine and study at

26. Bracket clock with pierced silver dial, silver winged Cupid ornaments and mounts. By Henry Jones, c. 1695

leisure a group which included many different styles of bracket and grandfather clocks of the late seventeenth and through the eighteenth century.

From the time bracket clocks became popular, a fairly wide variety of cases were adopted by different makers, but none of these seems to have represented a definite fashion except, possibly, the earlier forms of the basket-top, as it is called, which followed the first simple type and enjoyed a considerable vogue during the later years of the seventeenth century. Why it came to be known as the basket-top is difficult to say for the shape is formed of four sections of quarter round mitred—it might be described as a 'domical oblong' (24).

This type of case was variously decorated with pierced metal and eventually assumed an elaboration surpassing any of the eighteenth-century clocks. The first form was wood with applied pierced brass (occasionally silver) ornaments, the door being either plain (26) or similarly decorated (27). But the shape

27. Bracket clock with silver corner ornaments, mounts and vases. The movement is fitted with an alarum as indicated by the small dial behind the hands. By Richard Colston, *c.* 1695

entirely of chased and pierced brass finely gilded, seems to have been made about the same time (IX). Bracket clocks are also known where the case itself is veneered with tortoiseshell (XII), while in other instances the pierced top and carrying handle are of silver.

Two other styles of metal basket-top were made and each of these was more elaborate than the domed outline. One which is generally referred to as the bell-shaped basket-top has a more sinuous curve, baluster finial ornaments usually being added to each corner of the top of the case and pierced ornaments applied to the door and the frieze. The third type and by far the most imposing is the double basket-top which consists of a bell-shape with a flat platform surmounted by a domical section. The entire top is intricately pierced and chased often with a finial

28. Chiming clock with Turkish hour numerals made for the Turkish market by Markwick Markham. The case is veneered with tortoiseshell over-laid and inset with ormolu. First half of the eighteenth century

ornament at each corner of the top platform and the top of the clock case, all of which were gilded (XIII). Similarly elaborate pierced ornaments were applied to the door frame and sides and a finely cast and chased carrying handle fitted to the basket-top.

Having reached this splendour in the early years of their history, the cases of bracket clocks became simpler and passed through a series of changes which, toward the end of the eighteenth century,

showed deterioration in the designs. After the pierced basket-top
went out of fashion, the cases which are mostly without decoration developed from the inverted bell-shaped top to the several
styles introduced during the last quarter of the eighteenth and

29. Inverted bell-top case;
corner ornaments, the
crossed sceptres and crown
pattern with Cupids hold-
ing torches above in the
arch. Movement by
Christopher Gould, early
eighteenth century

early nineteenth centuries. The inverted bell (29) resembles the
lower section of the double basket-top, namely a domical form
rising in a concave member to a flat top to which the carrying
handle was fixed. This seems to have made its appearance during
the second decade of the eighteenth century at which time the
arch dial began to replace the earlier square shape (23).

Another style which is sometimes called the 'true bell-top'

(30) seems to have been introduced about the third quarter of the eighteenth century; this rises from the flat top of the case in a pronounced concave to a small domed top surmounted by the handle. From the few examples of this style, it would not appear to have been as popular as the earlier inverted bell-top described above.

During the last quarter of the eighteenth century, several styles of cases for bracket clocks were introduced, the more important of these being the broken arch, the arch-top, the lancet and the balloon. The broken arch (31) has a simple moulded arch top and obtains its name from the fact that this arch instead of extending the full width of the square case 'stops short' and finishes on each side in a narrow flat moulded section; and though

30. Bell-top case. Plain arch dial without corner ornaments; elaborately pierced hour hand, *c.* 1800

31. Broken arch case. White enamel dial with gilt corner ornaments, chiming movement by John Scott, *c.* 1775

32. Broken arch case with circular enamel dial; the arabic figures omitted except at quarter hours. Early nineteenth century

the more impressive arch dial with the silvered hour ring and ornamental spandrels or corner pieces was used with this type of case, it is more commonly found with a white enamel circular dial (31). Later bracket clocks in the broken arch case are much less impressive as the corner and arch ornaments were discontinued, the enamel dial being fixed to the case (32).

33. Lancet case. Plain enamel dial and wire-like hands. Note the lion head handles for carrying. Early nineteenth century

Each of the other three styles of the late eighteenth century is noticeably plain, indicating that with the more general use of clocks less attention was paid to the cases—and also to the dials which are invariably enamel. The arch top was a straight-sided case rounded to a semi-circular outline at the top to follow the curve of the dial and is often surmounted by an inverted bell shape with a brass finial ornament (34). The lancet (33) case is similar to the arch top, but finishes above in a pointed arch resembling the lancet windows of Gothic architecture; and the balloon (XV) also shows a close relationship to the arch top except that the lower part of the case is incurved or waisted.

While, as a rule, the bracket clocks with the broken arch cases were fitted with a carrying handle at the top, the handle would be sometimes omitted when a finial ornament would be added to the top of the arch and a smaller one at each corner of the narrow moulded sections which 'break' the arch. In such instances, however, a handle would be fitted to each side of the

34. Arch-top case with enamel dial. Note the entire omission of arabic figures. Nineteenth century

35. Nineteenth-century balloon case showing revival of the arabic figures

case for lifting the clock and that the 'portable' tradition associated with bracket clocks survived after clocks were in fairly common use is evident from the fact that many of the lancet, balloon and other late cases have a handle at each side.

During the nineteenth century, many 'novelties' in the form of cases for bracket clocks were produced, but there is no scarcity of fine clocks in cases of the old-time square type with the broken arch top which were made at least until about 1850. Unlike we humans whose value is generally regarded to be in inverse ratio to our age, clocks and other objects, when of good design and well made, increase in value—in terms of money—as the years pass. A clock made in the days of Queen Anne is a greater rarity than one made in the time of Queen Victoria; consequently a larger outlay is required to possess the former. But those of us who cannot indulge in the strictly 'collector items' may, with far less financial strain, acquire an attractive and accurate timekeeper in a broken-arch or similarly traditional case dating from the later eighteenth or the first half of the nineteenth century.

Considerable interest is offered by a study of the dials, hands and corner pieces of bracket clocks from the time they were introduced, particularly as these are to some extent indicative of the period at which a clock was made. As these features are similar in both bracket and grandfather clocks, we propose to devote a later chapter to describing their development and the several changes which occurred with them through the years.

CHAPTER NINE

THE COMPANIONABLE GRANDFATHER

ALL CLOCKS TICK, but a grandfather 'talks', and he 'talks' impressively. His small brother, the bracket, tends to clip his words and hurry his conversation while the later generation of the clock family with a lever movement gabble unintelligibly. In the room where this is being written, there is a grandfather whose slow soft voice is undisturbed by the chatter of the typewriter; and always companionable, he is never obvious yet invariably his 'words' blend with the mood of the moment.

When the mind begins to tire and thoughts and ideas are restricted, he seems to say, 'Don't press', 'Have a rest'; or if the sunshine pulls hard against work, that same old clock will admonish, 'Don't play', 'Get busy'. At the start of the day he stimulates, and in the evening when the curtains are drawn and you lounge in your pet chair, he says softly 'For-get', 'Re-lax'; and with his quietly persistent, but never monotonous, murmuring he brings a sense of well-being and pleasant detachment from the modern hurly-burly which is born of the thing we call progress.

He is not of aristocratic lineage, nor has he a long line of ancestors, but he represents all the various features which illustrate the evolution of his kind from the early lantern clocks which have been described in Chapter Six. A grandfather clock is to be found in many homes valued for its association with past generations of the family to whom it has come over the years. Often, too, that same grandfather stands silent and moribund for lack of some slight adjustment and so of little actual use other than to introduce a certain romance of the long-ago.

Nor is that the only romantic aspect associated with some of these time-tellers even if the additional 'romance' is of a material character. Many instances might be mentioned where a grandfather clock, which 'has been in the family for years' and accepted merely as part of the household furniture or perhaps neglected and allowed to remain silent, has eventually very appreciably increased the owner's liquid assets.

Here is one such 'find' with which the writer was connected—even if he were not the 'fortunate': He was asked by a mutual friend to look over some furniture belonging to a lady and decide which was worth keeping and which should be disposed of. There were several fine pieces in the house which, having been familiar with them since childhood, the owner regarded as of little value and had in fact put aside as unworthy of notice—several of these did not find their way to a country auction room but are now highly respected and, incidentally, equally valued.

In the corner of one room, unhonoured and almost concealed by other furniture stood a small clock. The very sight of it meant recognition and a warm glow, but to the owner it was, 'An old clock that has been in the family for years. It goes, but it's not worth much.' When this writer mentioned its approximate value, he was doubtless regarded as a candidate for a home where weak-minded people are cared for—later, when she had been convinced, the anxiety displayed by the owner proved how true it is that from ignorance our comfort flows. Previously, it was merely a clock that told the time; then suddenly it took the form of the wealth of Midas which had to be guarded and cared for. The first reaction to this was that the clock must not be sold, but shortly afterwards it changed hands for a sum well in excess of that originally suggested.

In describing this horological aristocrat, we purposely omit the name of the maker, for the clock is such a rarity that it could be identified with its present owner. It is only slightly over five feet tall with a small square dial which places it in the category of the so-called 'grandmother' clocks—a name traditionally applied on the assumption that grandmother, not being as tall as grandfather, could not wind the taller grandfather clocks, but had no difficulty with the shorter ones (XXIV).

Interesting as the small size of this clock may be, its real importance is in the movement for it is one of the earliest known examples of a long case which repeats the quarter hours. A light cord hangs from the side of the case and when this is pulled the quarter hours are repeated on five bells. A similar clock by the same maker was formerly in the Wetherfield collection, a fact which helped materially in the quick identification of its 'twin' in the house where it had long been unrecognized.

After which digression, we may return to the more plebeian grandfather that is recording the passing seconds in this room; while it shows nothing that would at first sight suggest anything of the earlier lantern clock, we may, by 'dissecting' it, trace its descent from that branch of the clock family.

As explained in Chapter Six and illustrated in (16), the frame of the lantern clock consisted of a top and bottom plate joined by four turned brass pillars with a brass door at each side, a plate at the back and the dial plate in front. Only two brass plates are used with a grandfather movement, one in front and one at the back which are connected by a stout turned brass horizontal pillar at each corner. The first movements, like the later lantern clocks, had the short pendulum with a small bob, the dial being square and quite small—about 8 inches.

As might be expected, examples of this early type are not numerous and while one of them is, at first sight, similar to later grandfather clocks, two differences are obvious, i.e. the square dial is much smaller and the case is quite narrow. The last feature is explained by the fact that the short pendulum swung in the hood of the case, consequently the case needed to be only wide enough to accommodate the weights. When, however, the long pendulum was adopted, this extended down and swung in the waist or trunk which necessitated the case being slightly wider.

It would seem that the first progression toward the all wooden case was the enclosure of a brass lantern clock in a wooden hood which was supported on a bracket with the weights hanging below. And it would be natural that this use of wood to cover the movement would suggest that the weights which were by no means ornamental could be similarly enclosed in what amounted to a panelled cupboard and so the first form of grandfather clock made its appearance (19).

When the anchor escapement (described in Chapter Five) and

the long or royal pendulum were adopted, the grandfather clock, as we moderns know it, became the standard time-teller in the homes of this country. In running order any one of these clocks is a reliable timekeeper and, if at any time it becomes slightly inaccurate, this can be easily remedied by adjusting the pendulum bob. The bottom end of the pendulum rod has a screw thread with a small nut; should the clock tend to lose time, this can be checked by screwing up the nut and so raising the bob, contrawise if the clock gains, the nut should be screwed downward thus lowering the bob. The amount of raising or lowering should be very slight and by watching the clock for a few days the exact degree can soon be ascertained.

As that now commonplace object, the pendulum, is very little understood or appreciated, we might here range for a short spell into the fields of explanation: If you look at the pointer in the small dial, usually in the upper part within the hour ring of a grandfather clock, you will see that it jumps one division or one second and then recoils slightly—the word 'second' meaning the one that follows or comes after. To ensure that each swing shall record one second, it was discovered that the pendulum had to measure 39·13 inches from the point where it bends the small piece of spring by which it is suspended and the point of gravity of the whole pendulum which is near to, but somewhat higher than, the centre of the disc or bob.

Therefore the pendulum of a clock of the usual grandfather type must make 86,400 swings to record the time accurately for the twenty-four hours we call a day. If the clock, at the end of that time, has gained, say, six minutes, it shows that the pendulum has made 360 swings too many or if it has lost that number of minutes the pendulum has made 360 swings too few. And each of these faults is remedied by the small nut under the bob by which the centre of gravity is varied—in plain language, the pendulum is lengthened to lessen the number of swings and check the 'gaining' or shortened to increase the number of swings to check the 'losing'.

One of our modern truisms is that demand controls the monetary value of an article and this applies to grandfather clocks with thirty-hour movements. Admittedly, it is slightly more trouble to have to wind a clock every day instead of once a week, but that does not detract from its ornamental qualities; and many of the thirty-hour grandfathers are as attractive as their more appreciated eight-day fellows.

When clocks were first enclosed in long wooden cases most of them had thirty-hour movements which were driven by weights on a strong cord. Many were wound in the same way as the lantern clocks, namely by pulling down the cords and raising the weights and these may be recognized from the absence of winding holes in the dial which are found with clocks which are wound up by a key. When, however, the going and striking trains were placed side by side instead of one behind the other, the thirty-hour grandfathers could be and were wound by a key and the dials of these have the winding holes.

It is commonly thought that the thirty-hour clocks were made only by the less experienced provincial clockmakers. Admittedly, the larger number of those which are still to be found in country houses, cottages and inns were the work of some local man, but examples were made by, now famous, London clockmakers. One by the celebrated Thomas Tompion in the Guildhall Museum has a lantern movement which is wound by pulling down the cords and raising the weights; another, by the same maker, which was in the Wetherfield collection, has the two winding holes in the dial.

After the long pendulum was introduced, it might almost seem that the more prominent makers vied with each other in producing a movement which would run for the longest period between windings. It is generally supposed that the maximum period during which a clock will run without winding is eight days. With very few known exceptions, this is true with spring-driven clocks, but as a result of experiments based upon close calculations several of the eighteenth-century clockmakers produced grandfather clocks which would continue going for a whole month and some are known which will run for three, six and twelve months. Any which will run for the last three mentioned periods are rare, but there are an appreciable number of month duration—there were upward of thirty in that part of the Wetherfield collection which went to America.

To achieve these longer going periods called for more intricate mechanism, a larger number of wheels and stronger driving power. This additional drive could be obtained with a weight-driven clock by using heavier weights, but it was impracticable with a spring-driven clock both from the point of appearance and the prohibitive cost.

While not a grandfather, a clock which strikes the hours and quarters and runs for a year without winding, illustrated by F. J. Britten, will serve to show how costly such a curiosity could be. It was made for William III by Thomas Tompion and is said to have been in the king's bedroom at Kensington Palace when he died. It was bequeathed to the Earl of Leicester and now belongs to Lord Mostyn whose family have owned it for some two centuries.

Tompion's bill for making the clock was £1,500 which has to be multiplied several times to arrive at the present day equivalent. The case which is of ebony with silver mounts, is in two box-like sections, the upper and smaller of which is similar to a grandfather hood with a dial, 10 inches square.

The lower section might be called the 'engine house', for it contains the two large driving wheels and the two powerful springs in the barrels with the accompanying fusees; and the many other wheels and pinions and the verge escapement connected with the striking and repeating mechanism are housed in other parts of this unusual clock.

SECTION 4
Curiosities and Novelties

CHAPTER TEN

ACT OF PARLIAMENT AND OTHER WALL CLOCKS

AMONG THE EVERYDAY things of bygone generations, there are many which expressed public protest or pleasure of their day: the potters had the best medium as is shown by the large number of figures of popular and caricatures of unpopular public characters; to a lesser extent, the silversmiths also expressed public sentiment in their work as in the little spoons decorated on the bowl with a bird escaping from its cage and the inscription *I Love Liberty* (the motto adopted by John Wilkes in his fight for freedom of the press, and the rights of electors to choose their representative without restriction); and the clockmakers contributed what is called the Act of Parliament clock (XXV), which symbolizes a public protest against an unpopular tax—which does not infer any tax is otherwise.

These rather ungainly time-tellers differ little one from another. As a rule, they have circular or octagonal wood dials about 24 inches in diameter painted black with the hour figures in gilt and a long rectangular or shaped trunk below, in which the pendulum swings; and with few exceptions they have the seconds pendulum similar to that of a grandfather clock. Probably owing to its large size, the dial is invariably without the glass covering found with other types of wall clocks, but while of interest for what they represent, it cannot be suggested that one would be suitable in any average home.

They are still fairly common in country inns and hotels and the answer to any enquiries regarding them is frequently that they were called 'Act of Parliament' clocks because they were ordered to be used in posting inns to time the departure of the coaches.

This legend, however, is more romantic than true to fact. For their origin we have to go back to the time of George III when tax-gatherers were almost as ubiquitous and as active as they are in our time, and when William Pitt, who was responsible for the introduction of income tax, was seeking more and more means to bolster the national finances. In 1797, he levied a tax of five shillings a year on every clock which, as they were then in fairly general use, meant a fairly heavy penalty on large houses. And Pitt or his legal advisers covered any possible loophole by which the tax might be evaded, for says the Act:

For and upon Every Clock or Timepiece by whatever name the same shall be called which shall be used for the purpose of a clock and placed in or upon any dwelling-house or any office or building thereto belonging, or any other building whatever, whether private or public, belonging to any person or persons or Company of Persons or any Body Corporate or Politick or Collegiate or which shall be kept and used by any Person or Persons in Great Britain, there shall be charged an annual duty of Five Shillings. . . .

Nor were pocket watches overlooked, those of gold being subject to an annual tax of ten shillings and those of silver or other metal, two shillings and sixpence. In addition, all those who made or sold watches and clocks in what is now the London area were charged two and sixpence a year and those in the rest of the country, one shilling.

To-day, these taxes would be regarded as merely nominal and certainly far from likely to have an adverse effect on the sale of clocks and watches. In 1797, a half-crown and even a shilling was an important contribution to the resources of the average household. The people refused to buy clocks or watches and many disposed of the ones they owned with the result that thousands who gained a livelihood from watch and clockmaking were out of employment. How serious conditions in the trade became is shown by the fact that within twelve months the tax was repealed—an example of the success of organized 'buyer-resistance' which might well be followed to-day.

In the meantime, for the convenience of their patrons and to attract others who no longer carried a watch or owned a clock, the innkeepers installed a large clock, of the type described, in the hall or some part of their premises where it could be seen clearly. And this was the real origin of these not-too-beautiful time-tellers being known as Act of Parliament clocks; not that all of them date from 1797-8 because they remained popular and were hung on the walls of inns for many years after; similar, slightly smaller clocks with white dials were not uncommonly found in the large kitchens of country houses during the last century.

But if these mementos of the famous Pitt are somewhat over-powering, there are other wall clocks which are suitable in a present day house and are easily come by.

Even when the grandfather was generally accepted as the standard family clock, either with a thirty-hour or eight-day movement, it did not replace the clock for hanging on a wall; the latter could be more easily accommodated in a small space such as would be available in a country cottage or similarly modest home. Those which are weight-driven are thirty-hour and are wound by pulling the end of the cord or light chain in the same way as the lantern and grandfather clocks without the key wind; the short duration of running time is explained by the fact that this allows for much lighter weights than an eight-day movement, and the clock would put less strain on a nail in the wall. This can be realized by comparing the weights of an ordinary cuckoo (about 2 lb.) with those of an eight-day grand-father clock (about 12 lb.).

It is probable that these country wall clocks will not be readily identified from the somewhat technical description, but when we add that they have fairly large white dials and often a convex glass with a long pendulum which swings busily behind the two weights, there will be less difficulty in recognizing what is commonly called a wag-on-wall clock. And, though the exposed weights and the pendulum offer temptation to a playful child (and when a draught tends to swing the ends of the chains or the weights, the family cat is apt to enjoy the fun), these clocks are excellent time-keepers and any inaccuracy can be rectified by raising or lowering the pendulum bob, as explained in the previous chapter.

One other type of wall clock which attracts little attention to-day, probably owing to lack of romantic associations or its plain appearance, is included here because it represents the continuation of that great tradition of English clock and watch-making to more recent days.

This particular English wall clock is familiar in offices as a plain white dial in a circular frame high up on the wall, at which members of the staff look often and anxiously for lunch time or the end of the day. Admittedly, not a thing of beauty, but any-one who has any knowledge of clock movements and has studied some of these office clocks will readily agree that they represent as fine craftsmanship as the movements of any period.

Some years ago we bought one for a few shillings and, as it was in need of 'first aid', did the necessary and fitted the clock in a more attractive case. As an example of an accurate time-keeper with simplicity of mechanism it is unexcelled. It is driven by a spring and fusee with a small steel cabled wire, the fusee having sixteen grooves; and provision is made against overwinding by a small arm with a click operated by a light spring—when the wire reaches the smallest end of the spiral on the fusee, it raises this arm which then meets a snail-like flange on the fusee and stops it from turning.

Clocks of this type seldom have a striking train, the movement consisting of six wheels and four pinions in addition to the fusee and barrel. The fusee, driven by the spring, passes the power through ninety-six teeth or cogs of the wheel at the larger end of the cone. These teeth engage a pinion that turns the centre wheel which engages a pinion on the arbor of the second wheel, the latter engaging a pinion on the escapement arbor. Outside the front plate, there are one large and two small wheels which, actuated by the centre wheel, operate the hour and minute hands. Actually it would prove an admirable 'patient' for an embryo enthusiast in learning the 'mystery' of first aid to clocks. And there is no more fascinating hobby to afford one a sense of achievement than the restoring of a sick clock to health.

In addition to the wall clocks described above, there is an early type with a wooden hood in every way similar to the hood of a grandfather and with these, like the wag-on-wall, the pendulum and weights hang below. It is probable that they were the English interpretation of the hooded wall clocks popular in Holland during the eighteenth century. Like nearly all weight-driven wall clocks, these have a thirty-hour movement and though most of them were made by provincial clockmakers, examples are known which were the work of men who became prominent members of the craft (XIV).

We should perhaps mention the so-called cartel clocks which belong to the category of wall clocks though one of them would demand a fairly spacious room to be 'at home'; nor would they have any great appeal to those of us who are inclined to prefer 'tailor made' to 'fussy' decorations.

Our modern word 'cartel' certainly has no connection with clocks nor had it any in France until it was adopted in the term *pendule à cartel* (later shortened to *cartel*), a style of wall-clock fashionable during the late seventeenth century. Incidentally the French word also means 'provocation' and it is not difficult to imagine that the fantastic and elaborate ornaments of many French cartel clocks would provoke anyone with a liking for 'visual quietude'.

Wall clocks of this type were made in England, but whereas the various figures, large scrolls, flowers and other, often fantastic ornamentation of the French prototypes were of cast brass or bronze heavily gilded, the English copies were carved wood, gilded. They have a plain white dial, usually with finely pierced hands and the movement is eight-day, as a rule, without a striking train though some of them both strike and repeat.

CHAPTER ELEVEN

SOME QUAINT HOROLOGES

THINGS, LIKE PEOPLE, are often the more interesting because they do not conform to the everyday pattern. Our eye becomes accustomed to and accepts any common type, but an object that departs from that type stimulates and arouses our curiosity; and this chapter is concerned with time-tellers which are 'curiouser and curiouser'.

At the outset, it is allowed that few specimens of any of them exist to-day and the possibility of acquiring one may be regarded as a hope which seldom knows fulfilment. But as will be seen, they demonstrate the inventiveness and ingenuity of the clockmakers through the centuries; in other instances, they represent either a small conceit or an experiment toward the achievement of some idea by an individual craftsman; again, it is equally possible that some were evolved by men who, though not professional clockmakers, were mechanically minded and played with the machinery of time as a hobby; and it is our hope that several of the last mentioned may stimulate the inventiveness of modern amateur horologists.

Nothing is known of the original contrivers of some of these novel time-tellers, but it is possible to trace others, among them that prolific inventor, Edward Somerset, 2nd Marquis of Worcester. This genius has been described by early writers as a 'speculative mechanical inventory'—a polite form of our more modern 'crank'. But looking back to his day, three centuries ago, it is clear that several of his ideas, which, at the time they were conceived, caused more smiles than they attracted notice, were later adopted and improved upon to bring fame and monetary reward to the adopters.

In 1663, he issued his little book, *Century of Inventions*, which deals with the details of a hundred of the more important children of his brain. And that his genius was later acknowledged is demonstrated both by the fact that the *Century* was reprinted many times and that a number of his projects came into general use. Among the inventions included in his book were: Telegraphs, speaking tubes and semaphores; explosive projectiles that would sink a ship; engines for dredging and raising ships; stenography, calculating machines, locks and keys and a steam engine for pumping water. This 'Water-commanding Engine', as he calls

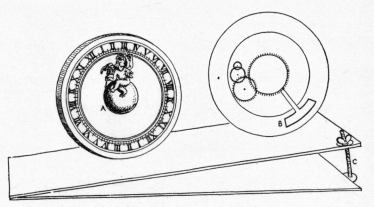

36. Rolling clock invented by Edward Somerset, 2nd Marquis of Worcester, about 1665. The method by which it works and details of its construction are described in Chapter Eleven

it, is illustrated in *Wonderful Inventions* (1882) where it is described in detail.

This aristocratic mechanic also came near to achieving that goal sought by many—perpetual motion. His contrivance consisted of a huge wheel with heavy weights which moved with the turning of the wheel. His own description is, 'that all the Weights of the descending side of the Wheel shall be perpetually further from the Centre than those of the mounting side yet equal in number and heft to one side as the other'; and this in modified form he applied to what was described by one early writer as 'an endless watch that never wants winding up', more generally referred to as the rolling clock patented by the Marquis a year or two before the *Century of Inventions* was issued.

In the Philosophical Transactions of 1684 the details of this 'Movement that measures Time after a peculiar Manner' are given at length and the illustrations shown here (36) are from the drawings in the Transactions. We will not repeat the prolixity indulged in by a Rev. Maurice Wheeler who, in 1684, apparently claimed to have been the inventor; the details can be summed up more briefly and more clearly.

One of the drawings in Fig. 36 shows the complete clock and the other the movement. The case is like a circular metal box 3½ inches in diameter and 1 inch deep and the hour circle is marked with the twenty-four hours of the day, i.e. I to XII twice. The centre (A) on which the little figure sits is hemispherical and rides loosely on a pin; the lower part of this hemisphere is loaded with lead to maintain the pointing hand of the figure in a vertical position so that it points the hour as the dial turns with the rolling of the clock.

It was worked by the train of wheels shown in the 'skeleton' drawing of (36). A stout arm with a weight (B) is fixed to the centre wheel and the clock is set in motion by placing it on a fairly long smooth slanting board when it rolls imperceptibly down the slope. It never requires winding, all that is needed is to place it at the top end of the board either in the morning or evening and like Ole Man River, it keeps right on rollin'. 'Adjusting the motion to the exact measure of an hour and rectifying its errors', as the Rev. Wheeler expresses it, or, in plain words, to regulate it was simply a matter of varying the inclination of the sloping board by raising or lowering the end with the screw (C) and so increasing or decreasing the speed with which the clock rolled.

Other later methods introduced to do away with winding were various and often quite involved, as for instance the remarkable nineteenth-century contrivance of weights and pulleys operated by expanding liquid reminiscent of the 'inventions' of Heath Robinson. Here we will be content to refer to some of the more simple 'self-winders' as for example the use of a small windmill driven by a current of air, the windmill being automatically stopped when the weight of the clock is wound as high as it should go.

Other novel devices evolved by the early clockmakers are

decidedly mystifying until they are explained. An unusually
ingenious form of these 'mysteries' was the so-called falling ball
clock which was invented some three centuries ago. It was a
gilt brass sphere hung by a cord from the ceiling much in the same
way as an electric light fitting, or from a bracket fastened to the
wall. The ball varies in size with specimens made at different
periods, though, as might be expected, any that have survived
are few indeed.

Round the middle of the sphere at its widest diameter there
was a band marked with the hours in two series of I to XII; the
upper and lower sections of the ball itself remain stationary but
the hour band is made to revolve every twenty-four hours by
small teeth on the inside activated by the mechanism enclosed in the
sphere. The cord by which the clock was suspended passed through
the sphere and was connected to, and wound round a barrel, and
the weight of the sphere and the movement pulling always downward turned the barrel and so supplied the power to the train of
wheels. When the sphere had dropped almost to the full length of
the cord, it was raised slowly upward by hand
when a small spring in the barrel caused it
to turn in reverse and the cord to rewind
round the barrel and be ready for the weight
of the sphere to again begin pulling (37).

One homely illustration comes to mind of
the simplicity of this 'mysterious' clock, i.e.
a spider hanging from the ceiling by his
web. If you touch him with your finger,
he immediately rolls up his web in his haste
to reach the ceiling and safety; then after a
while he 'takes off' and again suspends himself lower and lower. So as the weight of
the spider seems to uncoil the web—that of
the falling ball clock uncoils the cord from
the barrel, the cord, like the spider's web,
'disappearing' on giving the clock a slight
push upward.

37. Falling ball time-
piece suspended from
a bracket or a ceiling.
Invented during the
seventeenth century

British Museum

Another versatile titled inventor, Sir

William Congreve, is commonly supposed to have invented the first phosphoric friction-match (which is highly improbable as he died four years before it was introduced), but his fame rests rather on his war-rocket which was used with such effect at the siege of Copenhagen in 1807. And among the multifarious projects he conceived was a machine which he, like the Marquis of Worcester two centuries before, hoped would solve perpetual motion. And he, too, was responsible for a quaint time-teller.

In 1808, he patented a clock, which might be likened to a small table with the top pivoted to a pillar at either end so that it can be made to slope. This top—really a brass plate—is about 12 inches square grooved with channels in the form of what may be described as a series of V's joined, as it were, zig-zag fashion so that the channel is continuous. A small steel ball starts from the top and runs in the channels of the inclined plate until it reaches the lowest point. There it comes against and strikes a small release or trigger unlocking the plate which immediately changes its incline and slopes in the opposite direction, the little ball returning along the channels to the other side. There it strikes another trigger, the slope of the plate again changes and off goes the ball back down the slope.

Several models of this Congreve clock have been made during the past few years. Quite recently we saw one at Charles Frodsham & Co. and another at E. Dent & Co.; and, while watching that little steel ball running its seemingly endless journey, came the thought that the clock was possibly a 'by-product' of Congreve's experiments to achieve perpetual motion.

In the days when the standing salt was the symbol of social importance and the most important object on the 'borde' as the dining table was known, some of the larger ones were fitted with a clock; several were at one time among the royal plate as shown by an inventory and valuation of the plate in the Tower in the first year of the Oliver Cromwell régime (1649). This long list includes a number of great salts and among them '2 clocke salts standing upon 4 christall balls and 4 christall pillars each with aggatt salts set on the topp and gold covers' and 'a salte of state

I. The Dover Castle clock with original verge escapement and foliot with weights. The frame and wheels are of iron, the going train (right) being wound by the four arms on the barrel. This clock is believed to have been made in the early seventeenth century

II. Domestic striking clock of iron, the type known as 'lantern', with the original foliot balance and adjustable weights, verge and crown wheel escapement. Sixteenth century

III, *left.* Brass lantern clock with hour and minute hand, floral fret and engraved dial. By Edmund Massey, *c.* 1685

IV, *right.* Travelling clock in pierced silver case with an alarum and repeating movement. By Paul London, *c.* 1710

V. Circular table clock with large bell in chased and embossed gilt metal case, *c.* 1581

VI. Table clock with pierced bell-dome in engraved gilt case. By David Ramsay, *c.* 1625

Ashmolean Museum

VII. Musical clock playing twelve tunes, the titles of which are engraved in the arch of the dial. By Stephen Rimbault, c. 1780

VIII. Bracket clock, case of walnut inlaid with foliated scrolls in light and dark woods. Movement by Joseph Windmills, c. 1700

IX. Clock by Daniel Quare, c. 1685, in case with pierced metal basket top

X. Japanned case on plinth, movement by Daniel Beckman, c. 1700

XI. Marquetry case with movement by Claudius Duchesne, c. 1710

XII. Clock by Humfry Adamson, c. 1680, in case veneered with tortoiseshell

XIII. Pierced metal double basket top, with chased mounts on door
and sides, winged Cupid head corner ornaments, the arch engraved
with name of maker, John Shaw, c. 1685

XV. Balloon case with metal mounts and miniature.
Late eighteenth century

XIV. Small wall clock by Quare & Horseman, c. 1710.
H. 6 in.

Western Times Co., Ltd.

XVII. Clock with jacks at St. Mary Steps Church, Exeter

British Museum

XVI. Silver nef with clock by Hans Schlott, Augsburg, sixteenth century

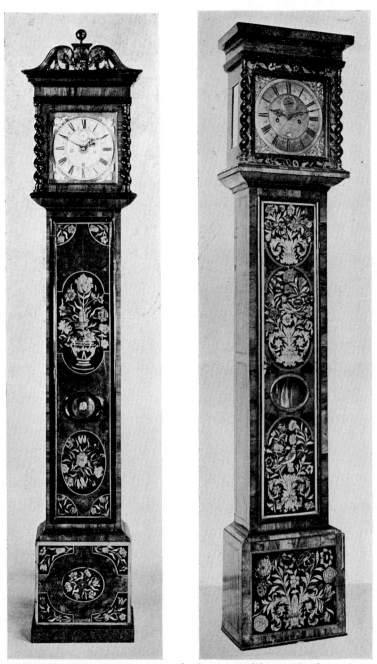

XVIII. Two marquetry cases with the more elaborate floral panels in coloured woods. Both clocks are late seventeenth century, one (*left*) by Daniel Quare and the other by Henry Massey

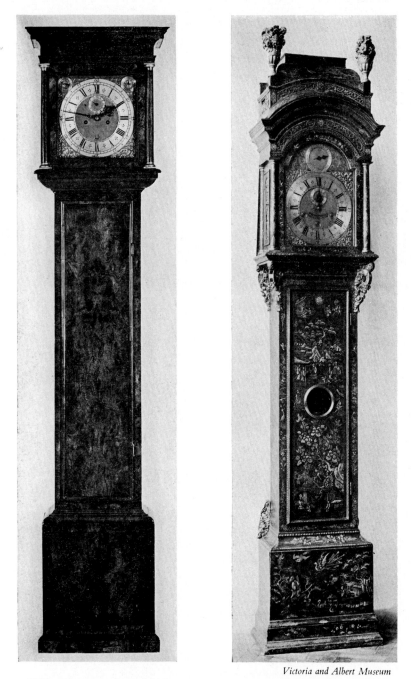

XIX. The case on the left is veneered with burl walnut, the movement by
George Etherington, *c.* 1710; the other is decorated in red and gold on peacock
blue lacquer, James Marwick, *c.* 1720

XXI. Dial of the clock by Thomas Ogden (see 54)
with a rotating globe showing the moon phases

XX. The dial of the clock by George Etherington. One
of the subsidiary dials (*left top*) controls the striking, the
other regulates the going part. Note engraving on the dial

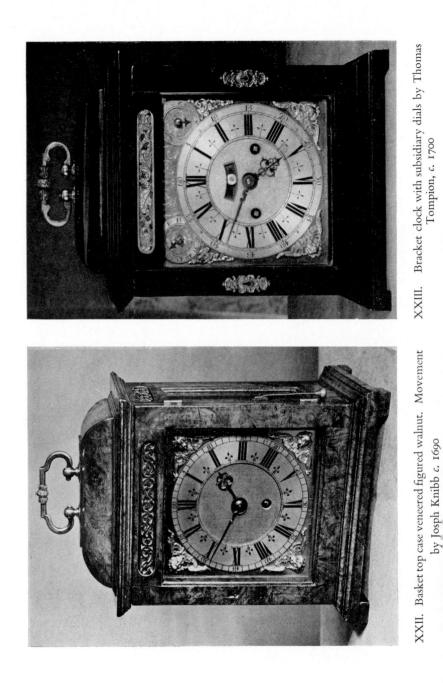

XXII. Basket top case veneered figured walnut. Movement by Josph Knibb c. 1690

XXIII. Bracket clock with subsidiary dials by Thomas Tompion, c. 1700

XXIV. The clock on the right, by George Graham, *c.* 1700, is
the normal height of a grandfather and is shown to allow comparison with the smaller clock by Christopher Gould, *c.* 1685, in a
marquetry case which is the size known as a 'grandmother' clock

XXV, *left.* Act of Parliament clock, wood dial

XXVI, *right.* Wall clock in ornamental case, *c.* 1760

with a clocke in it'; the '2 clocke salts' being valued at £77 and the 'salte of state' at £12.

While it is intended that this book should be confined to the work of the clockmakers of this country, we may in this present chapter range into slightly wider fields and touch upon some of the unusual time-telling novelties made by continental clockmakers. The various examples of German and French origin show that these men were particularly versatile and ingenious and we might here refer to a few that have been preserved and of which a number are in our public museums.

One of the most conspicuous tributes to the technical skill of the German sixteenth-century clockmakers and to the silversmiths of that time remain in those ancient ornaments known as nefs. These were models of a medieval ship called a nef and were fitted with various devices showing astronomical movements. During the Middle Ages one of these ornaments was the principal piece of plate on the high table in Germany though they do not seem to have been used to any extent in this country.

Some few have survived and an example which is in the British Museum is illustrated in (XVI). Measuring some 2 feet 6 inches long and nearly 4 feet in height this magnificent model is thought to have been made for Rudolph II in about 1580. It is in the form of a three-masted ship with guns run out at the portholes and the sails, rigging, crows' nests, housing and other features reproduced with extraordinary faithfulness. The clock which was made by Hans Schlott of Augsburg is at the foot of the mainmast and is fitted with ingenious mechanism which, at the hour, causes the miniature figures of the crew to move in procession.

There still exist in this country several ancient public clocks with mechanical figures, known as 'jacks' which were used even before clocks were fitted with dials; two of the better known examples are one over the entrance door of St. Dunstan's in the West on Fleet Street and one on the Church of St. Mary Steps, Exeter.

Of these two clocks, the St. Dunstan's is doubtless the more generally familiar. It was made by Thomas Harrys in 1671 and was the first public clock in London to have a minute hand; as

Harrys said in the specification of the clock he proposed, 'I will make two hands show the hours and minutes without the church upon a double dial. . . .' The 'jacks' are, as Harrys described them, 'two figures of men with poleaxes to strike the quarters' which they still do on two large bells. The two figures supposedly represent Gog and Magog who, according to the legend, were the only survivors of a barbaric tribe; these two were brought in chains to London and made to act as porters at the royal palace which was where the Guildhall now stands.

In 1830, the clock, Gog and Magog and several old statues were sold to the 3rd Marquis of Hertford and the clock was erected in the garden of his house in Regent's Park which he was then building and which he named St. Dunstan's, after the church. After the 1914–18 War, Sir Arthur Pearson bought the house and founded the well-known home for blind soldiers. In 1935, the house was acquired by Lord Rothermere who restored the clock to St. Dunstan's Church.

Exeter's ancient but less well-known clock in the tower of the old sandstone Church of St. Mary Steps (XVII) is probably about a century older than the one at St. Dunstan's in the West. The square dial is fixed to the wall of the church and above it in a recess with a Gothic canopy is a seated figure in Tudor costume between two standing soldiers each holding a spear; each of the soldiers also holds a long-handled hammer in his other hand and with these they strike the quarter hours on two large bells placed below their feet. It has been suggested that the central figure represents Henry VIII, but it would seem that even a sixteenth-century sculptor would have produced a better resemblance to King Hal than this statue shows. The three figures are known locally as Mathew the Miller and his two sons, Mathew traditionally being so punctual and regular in his daily tasks that neighbours could judge the time by the particular work he happened to be doing.

Similar automatic figures were adopted by German and French clockmakers to smaller timepieces and, though the figures themselves are somewhat rudely modelled, their many different 'actions' are remarkable. One in the British Museum is in the

form of a Negro with a dog at his feet. The figure holds a long
staff or pointer reaching up to a globe in an elaborate frame on
the top of what is intended to represent the stem of a palm tree.
The hour numerals in arabic figures are engraved on a band
round the middle of the globe which revolves and, as each hour

38. (*above*) When this clock is in going
order, the dog's eyes roll to and fro and
its jaw moves at each hour

39. (*on right*) Negro clock with which
the figure and the dog move at each hour.
Early German
British Museum

is struck, the head of the negro moves and the dog makes an
effort to jump (39).

Clocks introducing the Crucifixion with various moving
figures seem to have been favoured by German and French
clockmakers of the seventeenth century. A number of these have
survived to the present time and there are several interesting
examples in the British Museum.

One, illustrated by F. J. Britten, showing Adam and Eve in the
Garden, is particularly ambitious. It consists of three severely
straight, tall trees with foliage and apples. Each is surmounted

by a globe with a fairly wide band running horizontally round the middle. The globe on the centre tree is larger than the other two and the band is marked with the hours of the day in roman figures. One of the smaller globes shows the day of the week and the other the day of the month. A large and awesome serpent is coiled round the centre tree, its tail reaching to the top where it acts as the pointer to the revolving hour dial while its ugly head with the tongue extended is reaching menacingly toward Adam. Adam is shown holding up his left hand and as each hour strikes, Eve turns to him and offers the apple while Adam, tempted though resisting, moves towards her and then draws back.

Less intricate clocks with animal figures of which some part moves have also survived but these lack the attraction of the several automatic figures which, as it were, tell a story. One 'animal' clock the writer met with in America, probably made by a German clockmaker, is in the form of an unpleasant looking dog lying on a cushion (38). The cushion contains the movement and has a small hour dial and two winding holes between the legs of the dog which rolls its eyes to and fro when the clock is going and at each hour its lower jaw moves up and down.

If not a clock, the method of an eighteenth-century French abbot to ensure the monastery bell sounded at noon was simple and ingenious. Raising the hammer connected to a loud gong and tying it with a length of thin tow, he fixed a burning glass in such a position that at noon the focal point fell on the tow line which, fired by the heat, parted and allowed the hammer to fall on the gong.

In Chapter Three we described early methods of recording time by candle and lamp. While, as would be natural, these primitive time-tellers were discarded after the introduction of domestic clocks, several horological curiosities dependent upon a candle were made and used during the eighteenth and nineteenth centuries.

One which borrowed the principal of the sundial, i.e. telling the time by a shadow, consisted of a stout metal candlestick to which a long bracket holding a rectangular panel was fixed.

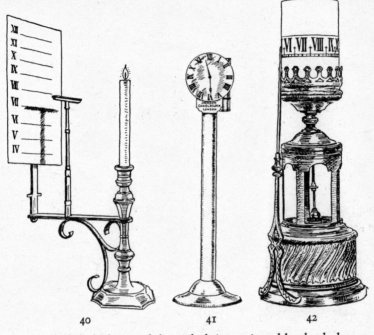

40. Candle-dial, the hours of the night being registered by the shadow on the card
41. Night clock. The hands are turned by a fan driven by the heat from a flame of a candle
42. Time-teller fitted to hold a night-light. The clock turns and the hour on the glass chimney is shown by the pointer

About halfway along the bracket there was a horizontal bar on a brass pillar forming a large letter T, the top bar of which served as the gnomon which threw a shadow on the panel. This panel was marked with a series of hours, starting with the earliest at the bottom. When a new candle was lighted, the flame would be above the level of the top bar of the T-shape. This would naturally cause the shadow to fall toward the bottom of the card or the earliest hour, then, as the candle burned down so the line of the shadow would rise to the later hours (40).

It would seem probable that this 'candle-dial' was the idea of some eighteenth-century amateur enthusiast. Again, it is equally possible that it was a serious attempt to produce a means of telling the time during the night; in the latter case, we may assume that the hours marked on the panel or dial would have been (starting from the bottom) XI to VII, thus covering a normal period between going to bed and daylight. Several obstacles would have to be overcome to ensure even approximate accuracy with this novel time-teller. Primarily, it would call for a fairly large and slow burning candle and it would be imperative that the flame be protected from any draught. Nor would it be a very entertaining task to ascertain and mark the exact place where the shadow fell on the dial at a given hour or half-hour as the candle burned down.

Another more practical illuminated time-teller was produced by Jackson of Clerkenwell about 1840. This consisted merely of a glass dial showing the hours fixed on a tubular candlestick fitted with a spring for raising the candle automatically as it burns. The hands were operated by a light flywheel which was turned by the heat from the flame of a special candle, the distance of which from the flywheel was kept constant by the spring pushing the candle up in the tubular holder against a nozzle at the top, the 'clock' being regulated by adjusting the flywheel (41).

Fig. 42 illustrates an unusually practical little night-clock which recently joined the writer's 'horologarium'. The movement is in the deep base and is ingeniously made to rotate a light crutch or guide, one end of which has a long narrow slot. The pendulum is suspended by a short thread to a hook and below the bob there is a thin 'tail' which fits and rides in the long slot of the rotating crutch. The pendulum therefore has a circular course and, as it rotates, the spring unwinds causing the clock to revolve on three small wheels in the base.

In the days when it was made and used, the holder was fitted with what was then called a glass chimney marked with the hours and quarter divisions, but that has long since been broken and cannot be replaced—the one shown in the drawing is a home-made 'chimney' of cardboard. A night-light was placed in the holder and the light from this made the hour figures visible in the dark, the time being indicated by the pointer which is fixed to a separate stand.

Placing the pointer separately was doubtless to avoid moving the glass when it was necessary to 'put the clock right', for instead of turning the glass so that the pointer is at the correct time, you merely turn the entire clock in the stand. It is fitted with a small screw to regulate it and at this moment the pendulum is quietly running its alloted circle (with a decidedly hypnotic effect if one looks at it for a few moments) and the dial records the quarter hours accurately—there are no minute divisions.

One charming novelty which was introduced to this country from the Continent is the use of a dial with a small movement in the tower of a church or other large building shown in a painting. These were popular during the early part of the last century and there are indications that movements by fairly prominent clockmakers were used in quite good paintings. One which is familiar to the writer was made by Harry Potter who had a shop in Aldersgate during the late eighteenth and early part of the nineteenth century and who was a master of the Clock-makers' Company.

It is set in the tower of a fine old church in a pleasant landscape picture measuring about 30 inches by 18 inches which was the work of an unknown but skilful artist. The picture itself is hinged to the frame and, by releasing a small catch, can be swung out from the wall to allow for winding the clock, which is wound from the back. This attractive little timepiece goes for eight days and the owner, who has had it for some years, says it keeps accurate time and has never been repaired,

Occasionally, you come upon a ship's clock with a striking movement and these are amusing to have in a house—and also quite confusing to the landlubber. Confusing because instead of striking the hours shown on the clock dial, they strike 'ship's time' which is one bell for every half-hour during each watch.

According to nautical custom, the twenty-four hours of the day are divided into seven watches, five of four hours each and two of two hours. Thus, starting from noon, a ship's clock with a bell would sound one stroke at 12.30, two at 1 o'clock, three at 1.30, and so on up to eight strokes at 4 o'clock. Then follow the two short or, as they are called, dog-watches, i.e., 4 p.m. to 6 p.m. and 6 p.m. to 8 p.m. the first of which should be sounded on the bell, 1, 2, 3, 4 and the second 1, 2, 3, 8. This is followed by watches of four hours during each of which 1 to 8 strokes are sounded on the ship's bell.

This variation is not made by the striking train of a ship's clock—at least it was not by either of the two owned by the writer—but carries on with one stroke at 4.30 p.m. two strokes at 5 and so on each half-hour till 8 p.m. when it sounds eight times, and this is the only hour at which the number of strokes agrees with the time on the dial.

Incidentally, time was kept formerly in the Royal Navy by hour and half-hour sand-glasses and this practice was continued until the early years of Queen Victoria's reign; thus do tradition and precedent linger, blocking the road to improvement.

SECTION 5
The Features We See

CHAPTER TWELVE

THE TYPES OF THE LONG CASES

ANY ENTHUSIASTIC ADMIRER of fine paintings knows moments of wrath, albeit silent, when showing some masterpiece to a friend, that friend expresses his lack of appreciation by the comment, 'What a beautiful frame'. And the owner of a fine grandfather clock may experience only slightly less irritation when his 'treasure' is commended with 'Isn't that wonderful wood!' or some similar banality.

Yet both the painting and the clock enthusiast should understand that others, not having their deeper insight and understanding, are affected primarily by what may be termed 'the immediately evident'. This, with a painting, may be a particularly brilliant or unusual tone of colour or finely drawn clouds or it may be the 'beautiful frame'. With a clock it is the intriguing burl (XIX), concentric curves of 'oyster' wood (45), the splendid feather design of mahogany (46), the vivid contrasts of lacquer, the delicate marquetry (XVIII) or any one of the elements of a grandfather which is immediately evident.

Its mechanism may be the acme of fine craftsmanship, the maker may have risen through the years to the Olympus of fame and one of his clocks may be highly valuable in terms of money; but as these factors are normally hidden—and, at best, few have sufficient technical experience to appreciate the mechanism of a clock—approval or otherwise is influenced by what is seen and, to some extent, understood. Therefore, it is natural that the average person should form an opinion of a grandfather clock from the case and the dial.

One late seventeenth-century writer, John Smith, in discussing

43. Plain narrow case
with plinth below base
and small square dial
typical of the earliest
grandfather clocks

44. Figured walnut case
with flat top and spiral
columns to the hood.
Movement by Thomas
Tompion, c. 1695

45. Case veneered with
oyster wood and cross-
banding. The hood has
the broken, pediment
and columns, c. 1690

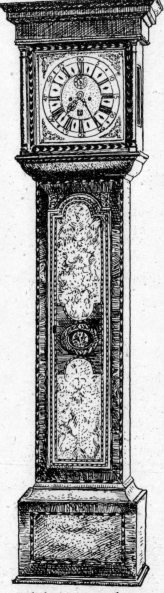

46. Case veneered with mahogany crotch showing certain features that are often ascribed to Thomas Chippendale, c. 1750

47. Irish late seventeenth-century clock in walnut case. The door and base panels are burl outlined with inlay; oval bull's eye showing pendulum bob

pendulum clocks refers to the method of 'setting up long swing pendulums after you have taken it from the coffin', the coffin referring to the early type of long wood case, a type which will call forth no feeling of admiration except from one who 'knows' clocks—others, it would 'leave cold' to use an expressive colloquialism. Incidentally, in former times, the word 'coffin' meant a chest or case and is closely related to 'coffer' which formerly had a similar meaning.

This writer recalls a case of this simple type in the Wetherfield collection dating about 1675. It was slightly over 6 feet high with a small hood, 12 inches square, a long waist only 9 inches wide and a base the same width as the hood. The door which was the full height of the waist was panelled like that of a small cupboard and the sides were also panelled. As time went on all these measurements were increased and there was a noticeable refinement both with the proportions and with other features which added much to the decorative value of these clocks as a piece of furniture.

When clocks were first enclosed in long wood cases, little attention was paid to the actual designs of the cases which were, for some years, of oak. But attractive as this wood can be for furniture, a tall, narrow coffin-like structure such as the early long clock cases, lacks either dignity or beauty. Then, as the grandfather clock came to be regarded as a normal part of the furnishings of a house, there was a demand for a more attractive case and the first move toward replacing the dull woodiness of the plain case was by concealing the humble oak with a veneer of ebony. While these cases gained some popularity in fashionable circles, the application of the ebony veneer was rather a distinction permitted by wealth than any aesthetic improvement.

Some of these ebonized cases have survived to the present time and are of interest as the first indication of the passing of the traditional oak and the coming of the more decorative walnut. The latter may be said to date from the accession of William and Mary in 1688, when oak was superseded by walnut for the cases of important grandfather clocks. And from the former simple panelled style, the cases of the later seventeenth and early part of the eighteenth century developed a sense of elegance which was unequalled at any other time.

If the earlier clocks are not as plentiful as those of the later eighteenth century and if those with movements by certain better known makers command high prices, an appreciable number of examples in cases of the walnut period have come down through the years. Various methods were adopted by the case-makers to achieve decorative surfaces and each of these has its own particular attraction. Where walnut was used, the door and that part of the waist which framed the door as well as the base were veneered with that fine figure known as burl, or burr. This is cut from some part of the tree where distorted fibres have been formed and which gives an indefinable mass of curly and wavy twirls dotted with dark brown spots rather suggestive of tangled wool (44, 47).

As a rule, the base was panelled with burl (sometimes outlined by an inlaid line of lighter wood such as holly) framed by what is known as cross-banding, i.e. the grain of the veneer laid transverse to the general surface; and in these instances the sections of the waist forming the door-frame were usually cross-banded (47). Another strikingly handsome surface was what is known as oyster veneer which is thin slices cut (as a rule transversely) from a sapling or small branch and produces a series of light and dark irregular concentric rings; actually the natural growth rings of the wood (45).

Beautiful as the walnut veneered cases are, they are surpassed for pure magnificence by those decorated with marquetry. And here, without trespassing too far into the fields of technicalities, it may be of interest to give a brief description which, for practical purposes, will define marquetry, parquetry and inlay; for though related, the distinctive differences are not generally familiar. Marquetry is a definite design formed of contrasting woods or other material which are dyed to obtain the various colour tones inlaid in a background of dark veneer and glued to what is known as the carcase which was usually of oak.

Parquetry denotes, more particularly, geometrical pieces of wood fitted together and glued to a bed or core. This is familiar in parquetry floors and the tops of backgammon tables; and it is the general practice to use the term 'inlaid' when the inlaid lighter wood is subsidiary and the greater part of the surface is the darker ground, as for example a mahogany sideboard with drawer fronts and perhaps the top outlined by a narrow strip of some lighter wood, technically known as stringing (47).

Marquetry, which was practised by the Dutch many years before it was known in this country, began to find its way to England in the form of furniture late in the days of Charles II, but it was some years before marquetry furniture was made by English craftsmen. The designs applied to clock cases might be divided into three categories: Geometrical shapes (48, 49) occasionally with a floral panel; floral blossoms and other forms in shaped panels (50, XVIII); and arabesques or other designs, mostly blossoms, which covered the entire front of the case. Marquetry was rarely applied to the sides.

Generally speaking, it may be said that the forms within each of these categories have the same basic origin. The geometric form most commonly used was a circular wheel-like shape with rays or 'spokes' in alternating light and dark wood radiating from the centre; and this may have been an occidental adaptation of the Buddhist wheel which was one of the eight symbols of the promise of happiness. It was variously interpreted in marquetry, but a common form is with wavy 'spokes' in a circle inlaid to suggest a scalloped edge or as a series of tapering 'spokes' similar to what is sometimes called a sunburst and not unlike the small fan-like wheel seen on the towers of wind-pumps. The usual arrangement of the circular ornament with a clock case was twice on the door panel (above and below) and once on the panel of the base, the angles of both panels being 'filled' by a quadrant of the ornament (48). Occasionally, too, a similar but smaller form was added above and below the upper wheel or sunburst.

In other instances, a small oval panel enclosing a vase of flowers was added to the upper part of the door (XVIII); and where this occurs, a wheel-like ornament is often added above and below the panel and a large star-like ornament on the lower part of the door and the base panel. Yet another style of what might be termed

48. Case veneered with oyster wood inlaid with geometric forms. Circular glass bull's eye in the door. Movement by John Fromanteel, c. 1680

49. Case decorated with fan-like designs in marquetry inlaid in oyster wood. Movement by Joseph Knibb, c. 1685

Frederick R. Poke, Esq.

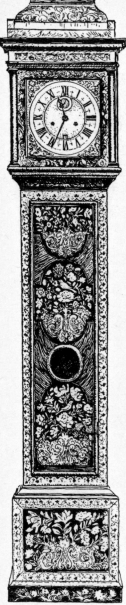

50. Marquetry floral
designs in shaped panels

the 'detached' marquetry ornamentation as distinct from the 'all-over' style,
shows a French influence in the use of
scrolls to form a more or less definite
outline.

Panels such as have been described are
relatively small so that the surface of the
walnut in which they are inlaid pre-
dominates. With cases where the
marquetry design is more elaborate, the
panels occupy the whole width of the
door and, generally, the panel of the
base (XVIII). Cases with what we have
termed the 'all-over' ornamentation un-
questionably represent the height of the
marquetry artist's achievement, as for
example, where the design consists of
flowers and leaves surrounding a central
vase, tiny birds and other motifs in mass.
Other designs, even more intricate, are
reminiscent of petit point needlework.

Though these clock cases ante-date
The Grammar of Ornament by more than a
century and a half, some of the marquetry
designs show a decided resemblance to
illustrations in that massive tome. And
for an appreciation of the more intricate
marquetry work we might well borrow
from that volume where, speaking of the
renaissance ornamentation, the author
says, 'in the majority of which grace-
fulness of line and a highly artificial,
though apparently natural, distribution
of the ornament upon its field are the
prevailing characteristics'.

There is no question regarding the
artistic qualities of the marquetry

decoration, but it is undeniably un-English in character. We call for suitable colour as a background to our furniture, but we have a marked preference for quite plain and no great liking for painted or multicoloured furniture, restricting the 'pictorial' additions to paintings, hangings and ornaments.

This native characteristic probably explains the decline of marquetry clock cases which by about 1725 were no longer fashionable. The finely veneered walnut cases remained fashionable, however, and at about this time clock cases were decorated with lacquer (and quasi-lacquer), possibly as a substitute for veneer, an appreciable number of which were made during the reigns of the first two Georges (51, XIX).

We have inserted 'quasi-lacquer' in the foregoing paragraph because the term refers to those often crude forms made of plaster applied on a ground of japan which is nothing more than one or more coats of paint and varnish. True lacquer which originated in China and found its way to Japan is a gum from the Oriental sumach tree, *Rhus vernicifera*, often called the lacquer tree. The gum when exposed to the air dries and becomes so hard that it will resist any solvent and it was this natural product which the Chinese and Japanese and, later, the European workers used for their groundwork.

Incidentally, only this ground-coating is lacquer, and not the pagodas, trees, quaint figures and other ornament which are applied on it.

Lacquered clock cases with movements by English eighteenth-century makers fall into three categories: (*a*) Those made and decorated in Holland and imported to this country; (*b*) those made and decorated by English craftsmen; and (*c*) that much smaller number which were made by English case-makers and sent to the Orient to be lacquered by Chinese or Japanese workers.

Any study of the lacquered cases shows clearly that the earlier examples are superior to those of after about 1740 when the 'novelty' had become widely popular in this country and quality gave place to quantity. In fact, for some years both lacquered and japanned cases were made in larger centres throughout the country and supplied to clockmakers working in smaller provincial towns and villages. And this explains why a grandfather clock movement bearing the name of a maker in an almost isolated rural district is sometimes found in a case more or less (usually less) artistically decorated with lacquer or japan.

More conservative people of the time, however, preferred the

51. Repeating bracket clock by John Ellicott, *c*. 1770. The case is decorated in the Oriental manner on green lacquer

'quieter' walnut which continued to be made for many years after the introduction of mahogany; the same may be said of oak cases which, in country districts, continued to be made until relatively recent times.

Many early grandfather clocks, mostly of the late seventeenth century, have a small circular (sometimes oval) piece of glass fitted in the door of the trunk. To those who have not journeyed to any extent into the horological realms this is somewhat of a mystery. It is known as a 'bull's-eye' and is more ornamental than useful, for, set at the level of the pendulum bob it was supposed to magnify the bob as it swung to and fro at the back of the glass (47, 48).

Actually the term 'bull's-eye' is associated with an entirely different craft, i.e., glass-blowing; and, as its origin is rather romantic, we might here indulge in a brief digression: Early window glass was known as crown glass which was made by blowing a mass (technically a parison) of molten glass to a large bubble with a blow-pipe. An iron rod, known as a punty or pontil, was then fixed to the bubble on the opposite side to the blow-pipe—the punty serving as a handle for manipulating the bubble, which was cut away from the blow-pipe. By spinning it rapidly like a mop in front of a very hot furnace the bubble burst and after a while expanded to a large flat disc or crown, as it was called. After being annealed it was cut into glass for windows, but that part that had been fastened to the punty was marred by the protuberance or 'bull's-eye'.

Obviously, the part of the disc with the 'bull's-eye' was far less desirable for window glass because, while it allowed light to penetrate, it was not possible to see through it. Consequently, its use was restricted to fan-lights, attic windows and outhouses. They are still to be seen in old houses and a complete 'crown' with its 'bull's-eye' was often used in a circular window frame in the gable ends of outbuildings or other high-up windows.

Before touching on the later eighteenth-century grandfather clock cases, a few semi-historical notes on mahogany wood will not be entirely irrevelant. Mahogany was introduced to this country about 1725–30, but though it became fashionable for furniture almost immediately, it was not used for clock cases until some years later. The reason for this was that until the middle of the century virtually all the mahogany wood was brought from San Domingo, Cuba. This particular wood was hard and dark-coloured with a somewhat monotonous straight grain devoid of any attractive figure, in addition to which it was both scarce and costly. Obviously, figured walnut would be preferred to wood of this relatively dull character, consequently the former continued to be used for clock cases for some time after it had been replaced by mahogany for furniture.

In fact, it was not until other varieties of mahogany were brought from Central America and the West Indies that the figured wood was obtainable and from that time walnut gave place to mahogany for clock cases. Most of the grandfather clocks familiar to us moderns have mahogany cases for the reason that as the eighteenth century advanced and these 'family timepieces' became cheaper, they were available to those with more modest incomes. And if one of the late eighteenth century with an arch dial does not inspire a connoisseur with the same enthusiasm as one with a small square dial in a figured walnut case, it adds much to the attraction of the hall or (across a corner) to the living-room, is an equally good time-keeper and its tick equally mellow and soothing.

To speak of a case as 'walnut' or 'mahogany' does not necessarily imply it is made entirely of either of these woods, but rather that it is veneered with one of them on a carcase, as it is called; the carcase usually being of oak, though many of the later ones made in the country districts are of pine.

As a general rule, in the case of mahogany, the door and base are veneered with the attractive crotch or other similarly decorative figure and the sides with straight grain—crotch is a plume-like 'design' obtained from the joint of a limb to the trunk of the tree and is particularly suitable for larger surfaces such as door panels (46). Here again, it is not uncommon to find provincial-made clocks having the entire case veneered with straight grained mahogany and frequently the base will be left plain instead of being panelled by the addition of a moulding.

Cases with certain features such as pillars on each side of the waist or trunk and the hood, scrolled pediments, bracket feet, fretted ornaments (46) and other forms of a Chinese character are commonly referred to as Chippendale; but while some elaborate drawings of cases are included in Chippendale's book *The Director*, there is no definite evidence that any were made in his shop; nor is it likely that any case-maker of that time would have attempted to produce one of those highly fanciful designs without first considerably modifying the original; and Chippendale's own conceptions would have little appeal in our time.

Thomas Sheraton, the erstwhile preacher who later entered the field of design, also includes some fantastic cases among the drawings in the second edition of his book *The Cabinet Dictionary* which was issued in 1808. No drawings of clock cases, however, appear in the earlier edition of 1803 and, referring to this omission, Sheraton remarks, 'as these pieces are almost obsolete in London, I have given no design of any; but intend to do it in my large work to serve my country friends.' But if his more ornate designs met with no great favour, his influence remains in the mahogany cases delicately inlaid with lighter wood.

Sheraton's comment that grandfather clocks were 'almost obsolete' was close to the truth, because at the time he was writing they had lost much of their former popularity, particularly in the fashionable world of London. They continued to be made in the provinces, and while the movements bearing the names of men in the smaller towns are excellent, there was, at this time, a marked decline in the designs of the cases. This was specially marked in the Midlands where the cases assumed often ungainly proportions and were embellished with a medley of unassociated ornaments.

How ungainly and ugly the cases of the North country clocks eventually became by the early years of the nineteenth century is shown by those usually bearing the 'sign-manual' of a Yorkshire clockmaker. These are unmistakable for they are upward of 8 feet high and 20 inches wide at the waist with the hood and plinth more or less proportionately wide; and this massive structure is often supported on ridiculously small bracket-type feet. These Yorkshire cases are frequently veneered with curly figured mahogany and inlaid, but while they doubtless attained popularity at the time and in the localities in which they were made, that popularity has never extended to the Southern counties, for at no time did these clocks attract much attention in the auction rooms.

We have dealt at some length with grandfather clock cases hoping to afford a more general familiarity with the progressive styles of the different periods. And something relating to the hoods as distinct from the trunk should be added to what has been said.

Before the introduction of the arch above the dial, all dials and consequently the hoods were square, usually with entablature and a flat top (44, 47) but sometimes surmounted by an ornamental pediment supported by spiral (corkscrew) or plain pillars, the spiral type being specially popular during the late seventeenth and early eighteenth centuries (44, XVIII). During the early years of the eighteenth century a dome-like ornament, some of which resemble the inverted bell-top used with bracket clocks, was added above the entablature (50) and this addition was sometimes accompanied by finial ornaments, one at each of the two front corners of the hood. The frieze, i.e. the narrow flat member immediately below the cornice, was quite commonly fretted to allow the sound of the bell to be heard more distinctly, and some of these fretted sections were of brass.

In passing, we might refer to the absence of a door with the hoods of some early grandfather clocks. To-day, when our family time-teller needs winding, we open the hinged door and use the key; but at one time the hood had no door but was made to slide upward in grooves cut in the back of the case, the hood being raised to a convenient height when it engaged with a spring to prevent its sliding down.

Speaking of hoods and winding, here a word of caution: When winding a grandfather see that the lower door is open so that you can watch the weights and avoid straining the gut after the weight has been wound high enough; otherwise it is likely to bring the weight up against the seat board with a jerk. This risk was allowed for by some of the early case makers who, by an ingenious spring gadget, caused the hood when it was down to be locked by the closing of the lower door.

And still another word of advice in the same connection. After winding your grandfather clock do not be satisfied by locking the lower door. Admittedly this protects the pendulum and weights from youthful fingers, but there is a greater risk from adult fingers playing tricks with the hands. So see that the door of the hood is fastened against trespassers. The hood door is not usually fitted with a lock, but one of several simple devices was adopted to prevent its being opened without first unlocking and opening the lower door. This is often merely a square staple or an L-shaped hook on the inside of the hood door, which passes through a slot in the inner frame where it is fastened by a small piece of wood—in exactly the same way as you might put a piece of wood through the staple accompanying a hasp on the shed door in your garden.

CHAPTER THIRTEEN

DIALS, HANDS AND CORNER PIECES

FEW THERE ARE in this disturbed world of to-day who, unconsciously perhaps, have not felt something of the magical spell and the eternal whisper which hover round the everyday things of the long ago. Maybe the past serves as a refuge from the commotion of the present; but whether the battle scarred walls of a medieval stronghold, an ancient Roman pavement, an early painting of some bygone scene, a screen in a village church, a massive iron gate made at a local smithy, or aught else, each 'resounds in fable or romance' and is a record of part of man's journey along the road to the culmination of his cultural development—and, it might be added, to the scientific iconoclasm of our own time. Yet, in seeing and admiring the handicraft of forgotten men, we so often fail to observe those minor details which, to wax poetic, are the tongues which tell the story of man's achievement.

Such details are many and various along the path of progress followed by the clockmakers and their associated craftsmen; and the domestic clocks of different periods, each serves as a signpost to guide the way. Admittedly, the technical skill expressed in the mechanism is not so readily apparent, but the artistic development is there for all to see in the dial or 'face' as it is commonly called—we might even vary a word to make the lines from *Macbeth* read, 'There's no art to find the clock's construction in the face'.

Here, for convenience, we are sub-dividing the 'more visible parts' of those clocks which are commonly met with to-day and which are suitable for modern rooms; therefore we may ignore the smaller portable clocks which are dealt with in Chapter Seven. Modern reproductions of the originals are obtainable and more will be said of these in a following chapter.

DIALS

If the dial of a lantern clock (16) is compared with those of the more accurate timepieces which came later, a marked difference will be apparent in the number of divisions and other details of the hour ring. The hours were almost invariably marked on this ring in roman numerals I–XII, the fourth hour being indicated by the more ancient four strokes IIII. This peculiarity persisted in modern times with clock dials where the hours are in roman numerals, though the IV was often adopted after the end of the eighteenth century.

No minute divisions were shown on the dials of lantern clocks, but the inner circle of the hour ring was divided to mark the quarter-hours, the half-hours being indicated by a fleur-de-lis or some similar device. There was no need for divisions showing the minutes because, with few exceptions, these clocks had only one hand, the 'pointing' end of which travelled round the circle marked with the quarter-hours. In those days, there were no trains to catch and life moved far more leisurely, so a few minutes were of no importance; nor was the movement particularly reliable as to the accuracy of the time it showed on the dial.

There is a difference of some interest between the hour rings of the earlier lantern clocks and those of the second half of the seventeenth century. The former are relatively narrow and the numerals which almost touch the quarter-hour circle and the outer edge of the hour ring have a somewhat squat appearance. Later, when a wider ring was adopted, the numerals are longer and there is more space above and below.

There was apparently no recognized rule regarding the size of the dial in relation to that of the case. The overall diameter of some of the rings was the same as the width of the front plate when the ring is flush with the sides of the case; in other instances, it was made a trifle larger and projected on each side. In the second half of the seventeenth century, the diameter of the hour rings was often noticeably increased in proportion to the case and in consequence the projection is greater; and toward the later part of that century and in the first quarter of the eighteenth century, the rings became so large that they frequently projected several inches which gained this type the odd name of 'sheep's-head' clocks.

Some excellent decoration was applied within the hour ring of lantern clocks and on the spandrels, i.e., the triangular space formed by the arc of the ring and the corners or angles of the front plate which, like the sides, were engraved with various floral or other subjects. The maker's name was engraved either within the hour ring or on one of the sides, but occasionally it was on the base of the ornamental fret above the dial—the frets have been described in Chapter Six.

Both bracket and grandfather clock cases illustrate the demand for more refined household furnishings which began to show itself during the reign of William and Mary and which developed to the dignified styles of the eighteenth century. And, in assuming a certain elaboration, the clock dials signify the improvement in the time-keeping qualities of the mechanism in various changes appearing with the divisions of the hour ring.

Until the introduction of the arch dial during the first quarter of the eighteenth century, dials of both bracket and grandfather clocks were square and almost always with a silvered hour ring. This carried on the tradition of the lantern clock.

After the adoption of the pendulum and greater accuracy in time-keeping was possible, the minute hand was adopted and the minute divisions shown on the dial ring. If, perhaps, the earlier bracket do not conform to quite the same definite style as the grandfather clocks, the features of the dials are similar and repeat the several changes which are more or less distinctive of different periods after these timepieces made their appearance in the later seventeenth century.

It is such seemingly unimportant differences that are helpful in approximating when a clock was made. The earlier hour rings are engraved with two circles close together on the inside and two others, slightly wider apart, outside the roman hour numerals— that is on the inner and outer edges (52). The space between the inside circles is divided into the quarter-hours and the half-hours marked by a fleur-de-lis, a lozenge shape or some device in the same way as the lantern clocks; that between the two outer

52. Dial of a late seventeenth-century clock by Joseph Knibb showing the minute divisions and arabic numerals in the outer circle, the quarter-hour divisions inside the hour ring and the fleur-de-lis marking the half-hours. Note the finely pierced hand and plain minute pointer, the seconds hand, the matted centre and the simpler form of Cupid's head corner ornaments

circles is engraved with the minute divisions and each five-minute division shown in arabic figures above the roman numeral: Thus above I the figure 5, above II, 10, above III, 15 and so on—and with the earliest dials, the arabic figures are inside the space formed by the two outer circles (52). Another quite minor feature which is apt to be overlooked is this: Where the arabic 5 is placed over the roman I the minute division is almost invariably omitted, but with other hours—being two digits—one figure is placed each side of the division (see 52).

Toward the end of the seventeenth century, the hour ring became markedly broader, the space between the two outer circles (showing the minute divisions) slightly narrower and the arabic figures above the roman hour numerals were then placed in the space between the minute circle and the outer edge of the dial (XIII, XX). The quarter-hour divisions on the inner circle and the device for the half-hour were retained, however, and though serving no useful purpose continued to be shown until about 1760. Instances are known where the minute divisions of the outer circle are omitted and the sixty minutes are shown by a series of arabic figures 1 to 60 but these are very few.

As the study of mechanical time-keepers advanced, it would appear that the more skilful makers sought to add mechanism that would record the calendar for the year, the days of the month and the days of the week, and these additions may have been responsible for the introduction of the arch dial. One of the first examples was the long-case clock made by Thomas Tompion in 1709 for the Pump-room at Bath. This has, above the square dial, a tall arch showing an equation dial marked *Sun Slower* on the left and *Sun Faster* on the right indicating the difference between mean time and sun time; and there is also a small oblong opening which shows the month and date.

Here we will digress and touch upon that somewhat mystifying term 'mean time' as distinct from sun or real time. One of the earliest items of knowledge we acquire at school is that the earth, moving from west to east, makes a complete revolution on its axis once in the twenty-four hours we call a day; also that it travels in its orbit round the sun once a year and so brings the several seasons. And it is upon these 'journeys' that time and all dials, from the first sundial, are founded.

In general terms, each day is defined by the regular return of the sun to its meridian or highest point which is midday. But, as the movement of the sun is slightly variable, time as indicated by the 'pips' and our clocks is reckoned by an imaginary or 'mean' sun which moves in the equator at a uniform speed based upon the average rate of movement of the real sun—the word 'mean', in this sense, implies the middle course between two extremes or the average. Equation of time is therefore the difference between apparent time as shown by the true sun and that reckoned by the imaginary or 'mean' sun which is familiar to us as Greenwich mean time.

This difference is variable, apparent or true noon, i.e. as indicated by the real sun, ranging from 16 minutes 19 seconds, in November, *before* to 14 minutes 25 seconds, in February, *after* the Greenwich 'mean' noon as shown on our clocks. The table of

the equation of time for the Greenwich meridian records that
sun time agrees with mean time—that is your sundial will show
the same time as your clocks—on four days of the year, namely,
about April 15, June 15, August 31 and December 25. On other
days, the sundial will be either 'fast' or 'slow' compared with
clock time and these differences are shown on an equation dial,
where one is fitted to a clock as with the one by Tompion
described.

It should be emphasized that the dates, mentioned above, on
which the sun or true time agrees with clock or mean time, are
approximate. The reason for this is the earth's journey round the
sun is some six hours more than a year of three hundred and sixty-
five days; which explains why each fourth year from the previous
leap year, an extra day is added to the month of February to
'absorb' the accumulated twenty-four hours.

There is, perhaps, something of interest and information in the
origins of the everyday terms we use to denote time. The word
'time' itself, like 'tide' is from the Anglo-Saxon *tid* (time) and the
Danish word *time* means an hour. 'Hour' which is descended
from the Greek *hora* (a season) came into use as the twenty-fourth
part of a day among the ancients during the second century, B.C.
—incidentally our word 'year' derived from the same source.

'Minute' and 'second' came to us, indirectly, from the trig-
onomical work of Ptolemy or, to give him his full name, Claudius
Ptolemaeus, the Greco-Egyptian mathematician and astronomer
of nearly two thousand years ago. In ancient times, all calculations were based upon the number sixty—known as the sexa-
gesimal system. The Babylonians divided the circle into three
hundred and sixty degrees or parts. Ptolemy doubled the number
of these divisions; he also divided the diameter into one hundred
and twenty parts, each of which he divided into sixty sub-
divisions, each of which he again divided into sixty equal sub-
divisions. The first of these sub-divisions were called, in the
Latin, *partes minutae primae* and the second, *partes minutae secundae*,
i.e., 'first minute divisions' and 'second minute divisions', from
which we derived our 'minute' and 'second' as applied to
time. Thus the hour ring and second dial of a clock are really

survivals of the ancient arithmetic founded on the number sixty.

When the arch dial first became generally popular and sup-planted the former square shape, it was regarded as a novel ornament or fashion rather than serving any useful purpose. In some instances, a plate bearing the maker's name was placed in the arch or it was engraved with a Latin tag. Somewhat later, the still familiar small 'Strike-Silent' dial with the movable pointer to control the striking train was placed in the arch; and during the second half of the eighteenth century, calendars, phases of the moon and moving figures were introduced to the arch of the dial particularly by country clockmakers (53); boxers fighting a never-ending battle, a ship rocking in a rather monot-onous fashion, or some other object was ingeniously attached to the pendulum and so made to move.

As a general rule, the phases of the moon are shown in the arch by means of a revolving disc, but some few makers, more par-ticularly in Yorkshire, adopted a rotating globe. They doubtless borrowed the idea from Ahasuerus Fromanteel, the seventeenth-century clockmaker who placed a similar globe showing the moon phases in a small compartment above the case of some of his clocks. The eighteenth-century grandfathers with this device were made largely at Halifax and are commonly called Halifax clocks. The one illustrated (54, XXI) was made by Thomas Ogden of that borough and probably dates from about 1750.

With the exception of those made for and used by the more prominent clockmakers, the dials of the later eighteenth century generally lack much of the high quality of the earlier dials. This was presumably the result of the increased demand for less expensive clocks both of the bracket and grandfather type. But —and this should be emphasized—even if the dial-makers and the men who made the ornamental corner pieces paid less attention to the finish of their work, the clockmakers produced as fine movements as at any time.

Therefore, a clock may have an enamel or even a painted dial instead of the earlier and more costly silvered hour ring on a finely matted surface; it may bear the name of some unheralded maker who carried on a local business in a small country town;

53. Yorkshire clock with
moving ship in the arch

54.   A Halifax clock by
Thomas Ogden (see XXI)

it may lack other refinements when compared with the much sought-for examples by well-known makers, but whatever its shortcomings, real or imagined, the movement was made by a craftsman proud of his work and it records the passing hours with the same accuracy as any by his more famous brethren.

Among the writer's possessions are two country-made grandfathers, each now about a hundred and thirty years old. One by C. S. Saddleton of King's Lynn is in a simple case of quarter-cut oak (cut so that it shows more variation in the figure) and the other by Mathew Harris of Bath in a case of mahogany veneer on a pine carcase; the latter is slightly more 'luxurious' as the door front is veneered with finely figured wood. We like to think that the first was once in the home of a prosperous yeoman-farmer and the other possibly ticked off the seconds in a house on one of the famous terraces about the time the bath-chair was superseding the more romantic sedan-chair in the historic old City of Bath. Admittedly, the dials lack the splendour of earlier clocks which bear the names of men now celebrated in horological circles; in truth the dial of each is white enamel with somewhat amateurish flowers painted in colours in the spandrels.

Dials with white enamel centres and gilded corner ornaments were used occasionally for bracket clocks (31) soon after the middle of the eighteenth century and from that time on they gradually replaced the former silvered hour ring; and during the later years of the eighteenth century and after, the cast and gilt corner ornaments were omitted. It was at this time, that white enamel centres were used with the dials of grandfather clocks even by the more prominent makers, while those by provincial men were either enamel or, where cost was a consideration, the dial would be painted.

Even if the later bracket clocks lose some of the former sumptuousness by the omission of the corner ornaments, they lack nothing in dignity or suitability for a modern room. Maybe a simple white dial in, for instance, a broken arch case (32), does not attract as much attention, but it is a charming addition to any room whether placed on the mantel or a table; and moreover, such a clock does not demand any very heavy call on the family purse—which is admittedly a rationalisation, for those early eighteenth-century bracket clocks are so very desirable.

That beauty which comes from fine proportions was maintained with bracket clocks until modern times, but grandfather in the early nineteenth century and later came to know some descendants whose 'bodies' were malformed and disproportionate and whose 'faces' were far from handsome. Many of these were 'born' in the north of England and seem to have been especially popular in Yorkshire where large circular dials, usually painted, were fitted into the massive cases described previously; and the hour numerals of these dials are often in arabic figures.

Fortunately such cumbersome and unattractive 'structures' are exceptional, for like the bracket clocks, grandfathers retained what may be called their friendly features which, generally speaking, distinguish them and which explains the affection which most of us know toward the one whose mellow whisper in the hall or the corner of a room confers an atmosphere of peace and freedom from the daily round.

HANDS

Most of the original forms composing what we call design came from Nature. This is evident in the names applied to various constructional elements more particularly in cabinet-making. One may quickly call to mind a considerable list of shapes and names familiar in furniture which were borrowed from human and animal anatomy ranging from arm to toe and hock to lion mask. In the potters' and silversmiths' crafts there are the horn-shape, the pear, gourd and others while the decoration of pottery and silver are also natural forms. With clocks which are basically the cycle of the sun, there is the grasshopper escapement, the snail, the jaws, we commonly refer to the dial as the 'face' and a clock has hands.

This use of the word 'hand' for a pointer indicating the hour has a more natural derivation than might be generally thought. With early clocks, the pointer or indicator was the shape of a hand with the index finger extended, as commonly seen on signs and some old roadside sign-posts in our time. The clock hand was cut from light metal either with the additional length of 'arm' or fixed to a separate piece of metal; and at the Victoria and Albert Museum, there is a German late fifteenth-century clock with an indicator of this type.

Carl Drepperd in his *American Clocks and Clockmakers*, mentions that when the hand of a clock was actually in the form of a human

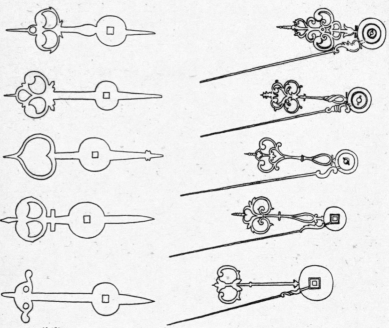

55a.   (*left*) Some types of the single hands used with lantern clocks during the seventeenth century

55b.   (*right*) Late seventeenth-century hour hands developed from the earlier lantern clock hands after the introduction of the minute hand which, at first, was a plain pointer

hand, the curiously awkward term 'hand-hand' was sometimes used to denote this feature and that 'hand-hands' are found with some American tall clocks of the eighteenth century.

As is to be expected, the lantern clock hand is simpler than those of the bracket and grandfather clocks. The 'hand-hand' pointer was soon replaced by the fleur-de-lis and something of this outline can be seen in the hands of the first English domestic timepieces.   Several of the types used with lantern clocks are illustrated in (55a).   The fleur-de-lis outline is traceable in the simple form with two scroll 'ears' (55a) and again in the more sophisticated shapes in each of which the head of the pointer is finely shaped while the perforations are larger and more artistic.

Some hands are referred to as 'spade-head', as for example those

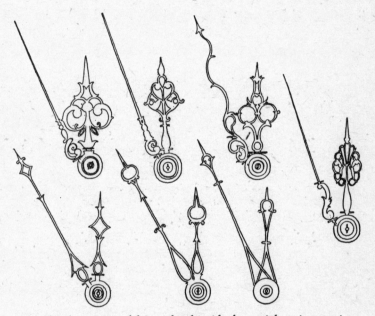

56.   The three more elaborate hands with the straight minute pointer illustrate types used during the eighteenth century until about 1760; the one with the 'squiggly' minute hand appeared about 1780 and the insignificant forms below, about 1790

shown in (55a).   While it is not easy to see the shape of the garden tool in these clock hands, the seemingly useless little cross-bar (55a) may possibly be a relic of the Greek *pala* or spade; the *pala* had a long D-shaped blade with a cross-bar above for pressing it into the ground with the foot.

Until the later years of the eighteenth century, when machinery began to replace handicraft, all clock hands were cut out by hand and carefully filed and finished.   Consequently, as time went on and there was a greater demand for more ornamental hands, the craftsmen vied with each other in producing intricately perforated shapes. This, however, applies more to those of the bracket and grandfather hands as we shall see in the following paragraphs, for while the later lantern clock hand developed a certain ornamental quality, the simplicity remains dominant until the late eighteenth century when shapes and pierced designs similar to those of the hour hand of contemporary bracket and grandfather (56) were adopted.

Some few examples of quite early bracket and grandfather clocks fitted with only one hand like their predecessor the lantern are still known; but the progression of clock hands can be followed in those which appeared during and after the last ten years of the seventeenth century. With the introduction of the pendulum in about 1660, it was not long before the minute hand was adopted and, soon after, the second hand with the familiar small dial was added.

As the development of the hands for bracket and grandfather clocks was to all intents the same, the following details will serve equally for both. If the hands of a clock made before about 1760 are compared with those of one made after that time, one obvious difference will be seen in the style of the minute hands. With the pre-1760 clock, the minute hand is merely a plain thin pointer with a small scroll at the base and unrelated to the hour hand (55b, 56); after that time, both hands tend to be more and more similar in design (56). Then from about 1790 when clock hands began to be stamped out, both are the same style differing only in length, the former finely pierced forms disappear and give place to insignificant and tawdry lozenge or other geometric shaped pointers with looped shanks (56).

Clock hands not only indicate the time of day (if the movement is in going order) but within certain limits also indicate the approximate period at which a clock was made. From the time when the minute hand was adopted, they may be classified under four general groups, each representing a more or less definite period. It should be noted that we say 'four general groups', because, before the introduction of stamped hands, they were hand-made and the details of the design of the hour hand vary according to the idea of the individual designer and maker.

Until about 1690, the hour hand is almost invariably a more advanced form of the double loop developed from that of the lantern clock (compare 55a and 55b). This type may be said to be two C-scrolls, one reversed, with a pointer, and is often reminiscent of the quite early fleur-de-lis hand which, as we have said, followed what has been referred to as the 'hand-hand'; this fleur-de-lis appears in (55b, lower figure). Gradually the original double loop outline is elaborated by the addition of more scrolls until designs such as shown in (55b) develop.

This elaboration was further extended and during approximately the last ten years of the seventeenth century, the hands are noticeably larger and the pierced work particularly intricate; and the minute hands of this period begin to become more ornamental by the addition of larger scrolls to the base though the plain straight pointer is retained (55b). After about 1710, the hour hands tend to become smaller, but with slightly longer shanks, and the pierced designs gradually become less intricate.

After about 1750–5, the designs become stereotyped, the hands themselves being noticeably longer; later the minute hand takes a 'squiggly' shape with several tiny protruding spikes (56), though the former straight pointer with the scroll at the base continued to be used. After about 1790, as mentioned previously, the hands were debased to skinny wire-like forms such as would be produced by mechanical means and consequently lack any of the artistry which had distinguished the early hand-made examples.

SPANDREL ORNAMENTS

As we have seen, the features of bracket and grandfather clocks were evolved from those of the brass lantern clock, though perhaps in their final development, the relationship is not always apparent. But, as it is possible to follow the development of the dials and hands, so it is to see the original suggestion of the later applied corner or spandrel ornaments in the decoration of the lantern dial plates.

With the silvered ring of the latter applied to the rectangular front plate, the spaces formed by the arc of the ring and the angles of the plate (known as spandrels) were merely a plain surface. To tone down this sense of bareness, the spaces were engraved with some floral or other ornament (III) and, when the dial was so placed as to leave a space below, that space was also engraved.

This method of decorating brass clock cases was used by continental makers long before domestic clocks came into general use in this country, one of the earliest known English examples being a small brass clock made by Bartholomew Newsam in the British Museum and referred to in Chapter Seven.

For a short while after clocks in wooden cases made their appearance, some of the spandrels were engraved, but this was soon superseded by the gilt corner pieces. These ornaments were cast in brass, finely tooled and gilded and fixed to the dial plate, the first pattern being a cherub's head with wings (57). It would seem probable that this was introduced about 1670 as the clock in the coat of arms of the Clockmakers' Company (granted 1671) has this form of ornament.

These simpler winged cherub ornaments remained popular with bracket clocks for some years after but they were replaced by larger and more elaborate designs (57) with grandfather clocks in about 1680. During the time of Queen Anne, designs which might suggest a tribute to the reigning monarch were used by some clockmakers. One of these was two Cupids holding a crown (59), another similar form was two winged Cupids kneeling, each holding a sceptre and supporting a crown. Gilt brass ornaments, of a character similar to those applied to the spandrels, were also used on the arch when the arch dial replaced the earlier square shape.

After about 1750, when the rococo influence impressed itself upon English design, the chubby little Cupids disappear and the designs develop a foreign feeling due to the free use of scrolls (58). These and other 'fussy' forms continued to be used through the reign of George III, one, which was popular during the later years of the eighteenth century, being a female

57.   Spandrel or corner ornaments for dials.   The Cupid's head
with wings was adopted about 1670 and soon after that time
more ornamental scrollwork was added to the winged head

head as the centre of an elaborately foliated scroll design (58).
Except for those clocks by more prominent makers, the later
spandrel ornaments are not comparable either in design or finish
with those of the earlier examples; and after the end of the
eighteenth century with the more general use of enamel and
painted dials, the spandrels were decorated with a painted flower
or other simple motif. Gilt brass ornaments were also used with

58.   Others, also showing the rococo influence, became fashionable and replaced the Cupid after about 1750

both bracket and grandfather clocks having circular painted dials
during the last quarter of the eighteenth century, the design
generally being that shown in (31); instances of this are relatively
rare however.

    To note the various details of grandfather clock dials is to find
that at least some of the early makers had a sense of humour. This
finds expression in the different mottoes inscribed on the dials—
and the fact that both these mottoes and the maker's name were

frequently in Latin might suggest that they also had a desire to appear erudite.

Over the years, the writer has assembled a number of these mottoes, many of which were derived from Horace, Virgil, Ovid and other ancient writers for they include: *Fugit irreparabile tempus* (Time is flying never to return); *Tempus anima rei* (Time is the soul of business); *Tempus omnia revelat* (Time reveals all things) and that very pointed hint, *Tempus abire tibi est* (It is time for you to leave).

59. Two Cupids holding a crown amid scrollwork

CHAPTER FOURTEEN

A SUMMARY OF THE DEVELOPMENT OF MECHANICAL CLOCKS

THOUGHTS AND IDEAS are like birds—they come unexpectedly and disappear as quickly. Which is why there is on this desk a book in a vivid scarlet cover labelled 'Jottings'. It receives thoughts direct or from a piece of board or even slate on which they have been scribbled when working at the bench or in the garden.

Among the scribbles and hieroglyphical drawings is a rough 'genealogical tree' of the clock family. It was intended as a helpful pictorial continuity chart in preparing this book. The publishers, after reading the typescript, suggested a summary of the salient features for dating and placing—for which suggestion, many readers will be and the writer is grateful.

In this summary and the chart shown, we need deal only with the 'original ancestor' of English mechanical clocks, his immediate descendants and the two later main branches, i.e., the weight-driven and the spring-driven clocks. There were a number of miscellaneous offshoots, of which many are described in Section Four.

1. THE ORIGINAL was the massive iron public clock such as the one shown in (I). Made entirely of iron by blacksmiths, it has only one wheel which is turned or driven by the pull of the weight on the stout rope. This drives a pinion (small wheel) on the vertical escape wheel (sometimes called a crown wheel), the triangular shaped teeth of which escape alternately from the pallets (small projections) on the verge (vertical shaft) which turns backward and forward with the swing of the foliot (the bar at the top with a weight on each of the L-shaped ends) (11a).

2. FIRST DOMESTIC (LANTERN) CLOCK: Sixteenth century. A miniature of the large public clock. Similar verge escapement and foliot. One hand, gong above. Sides and back open. Pull-up wind. Entirely of iron. (II).

3. BRASS LANTERN CLOCK, c. 1605. Verge escapement and foliot. Movement enclosed by brass back plate, door at each side and front plate. Brass wheels, silvered hour ring; front plate and sides engraved. Ornamental frets at top of case varying in design at different periods (57-59). One hand, gong above. Thirty-hour weight driven movement. Pull-up wind.

4. LANTERN CLOCK, c. 1620. Verge escapement and balance wheel (replacing foliot). Brass case with frets above. Silvered hour ring. One hand, gong above. Thirty-hour weight-driven movement. Pull-up wind. Many with balance wheel (11b) later converted to pendulum.

5. LANTERN CLOCK, c. 1660. Verge and escape wheel fitted horizontally at top of clock. Short pendulum with small bob fixed to end of verge. Swing of pendulum lifts pallets as was done previously by movement of foliot. Brass case, frets, hour ring, thirty-hour duration and pull-up wind as before. Pendulum occasionally fitted to swing in front of dial.

6. LANTERN CLOCK, c. 1660-5. Verge escapement and short pendulum as in No. 5. Weight-drive replaced by spring barrel and fusee drive (13). Wound by turning fusee with key. Substitution of spring for weights allowed the clock to stand on a mantel or a table instead of hanging from a wall or being placed on a bracket.

7. BRACKET CLOCK, c. 1665. The lantern clock movement (No. 6) in a wood instead of a brass case. The verge escapement and spring and fusee drive with short pendulum continued in use with bracket clocks after the anchor escapement and longer pendulum with heavier disc were adopted with weight-driven clocks. Anchor escapement and longer pendulum more generally used with bracket clocks after about 1710. Various styles of cases at different periods through the late seventeenth and eighteenth centuries. Earliest cases were architectural in style; basket top variously ornamented with pierced metal during the late seventeenth century. Eighteenth-century cases simpler (see Chapter Eight). Dials, hands and corner pieces vary at different periods (see Chapter Thirteen).

8. FIRST LONG CASE OR GRANDFATHER CLOCK, c. 1665. The

weight-driven lantern movement, as in No. 5, was enclosed in wooden hood and hung on wall with the weights exposed below. Then the weights were enclosed in a cupboard-like case. Some of the thirty-hour grandfather clocks wound by pulling up weights which were suspended on stout cord; others wound by key when weights were suspended on gut line which coiled round a winding barrel. With the key wind, the arbor (axle) of each barrel extends to a winding hole in the dial. One or two hands. Small square dial.

No. 9. EIGHT-DAY GRANDFATHER CLOCK, c. 1675. Anchor escapement with long (seconds) pendulum. By varying the mechanism, the more skilled makers also produced grandfather clocks which would require winding once a month, once in three months or even twelve months. Two hands and second hand. Earliest cases plain oak. From late seventeenth century decoration added by veneers, marquetry, lacquer. Features, distinctive of more or less definite periods, occurring with the cases, dials, hands and corner pieces are described in Chapters Twelve and Thirteen.

Small portable timepieces are distinct from those summarized above. They were made during the sixteenth century after the invention of the spring barrel and fusee. Examples by English clockmakers are very rare. See Chapter Seven.

W. Large iron public clock with vertical verge escapement and foliot (I) probably fifteenth century

W. Iron chamber (lantern) clock with vertical verge and foliot (II) late sixteenth century

W. Brass lantern with vertical verge and foliot. c. 1665

S. Modern reproduction brass lantern with lever movement (62)

S. Lantern with horizontal verge, short pendulum, spring barrel and fusee drive. c. 1660–65 (13)

Movement enclosed in wood case

S. Bracket clock in wood case, anchor escapement, long pendulum, heavier disc. Square or, later, arch dial. c. 1710

S. Modern reproduction bracket clock with lever movement. (67, 68)

W. Lantern with vertical verge and balance wheel. c. 1620 (11b)

W. Lantern with horizontal verge and short pendulum with light bob. c. 1660

Movement enclosed in hood with and without case below

S. Bracket clock in wood case with horizontal verge, short pendulum, barrel and fusee drive. Square dial. c. 1665

W. Wall clock in hood, exposed weights below. c. 1665 (XIV)

W. Thirty-hour long case (grandfather) with verge and short pendulum. Pull-up or key wind. Square dial. One or two hands. c. 1665

W. Eight day or longer period grandfather with anchor escapement and long (seconds) pendulum. Square dial. c. 1675

W. Ditto with arch dial. c. 1720

W. Modern reproductions of both square and arch dial styles

Dates: Approximate commencement of type.
W.—driven by weights
S.—driven by spring

SECTION 6
The New From The Old

CHAPTER FIFTEEN

MODERN REPRODUCTIONS OF EARLY CLOCKS

WHEN MECHANICAL TIME-TELLERS first appeared, they were largely the work of the blacksmith and some four hundred years later it was the son of a blacksmith who ruffled the then powerful English clockmaking trade; and he also proved that clocks could be produced at a price which would be within the reach of even the cottage home.

This revolutionary disturber, Chauncey Jerome of Plymouth, Connecticut, had a varied career before arriving at the goal of his eventual success: When he was nine years old, he worked in his father's forge; two years later, he was on a farm where he seems to have remained until he was fifteen. He was then apprenticed to a carpenter for six years, but, before he had served his time, was released to work for a maker of clock dials from which he later graduated to making clocks and cases.

In about 1838, he conceived an idea for a cheap small one-day clock with brass wheels and invented a machine for cutting the wheels. With this machine, he was able to make clocks on a mass production scale and to sell them at a price which created so wide a demand that he was soon selling thousands in his native country.

Looking for new fields to conquer, in 1841, he sent a consignment of his small clocks to England. The English Customs authorities, when they saw the low price at which the clocks were invoiced, quickly realized the effect on the home trade if these American clocks were offered for sale in England. They insisted that Jerome had undervalued them, but Jerome was equally insistent that the price was correct, so to safeguard the home industry (perhaps thinking to call the American's bluff) the English Government bought the entire shipment and paid for it.

But Jerome was not bluffing. Finding such a ready sale free of any selling costs, he promptly sent over another and larger consignment. Again the English Government purchased the

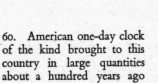

60. American one-day clock of the kind brought to this country in large quantities about a hundred years ago

shipment much to the delight of the American clockmaker who continued to send over his products in always increasing numbers. This might be regarded as the first instance of 'government bulk buying' and the Treasury continued to pass payment. In time, someone must have woken up and decided that the stock in the national clock-shop was becoming unwieldy. At long last the British authorities, realizing that Jerome intended to continue his shipments, admitted defeat and the clocks were soon being distributed and sold freely throughout this country.

Many of those small clocks survive to the present time and it is by no means uncommon to see one on the mantel-shelf of a country cottage or in a small antique shop. The cases are wood with either a plain flat top or a pointed arch and a conical shaped pinnacle or a turned finial on each side. The lower part of the door is usually a glass panel decorated with a landscape or other subject. An example is shown in (60).

Since that time, fashions in clocks have passed through many phases. There was the vogue of the weird skeleton with its massive marble base and huge glass dome, dear to the Victorian mother and father both as a possession and as a wedding gift. And there are yet those of us who can recall the punishment threatened to any who should dare to lift that glass dome—a

61. A form of timepiece representative of the eccentricities of the so-called Empire style, fashionable in the early nineteenth century

sacred office reserved to Father or the clock-winder who solemnly went from room to room each week, regulating and winding the family time-tellers.

And there are drawing-rooms (not many, 'tis true) remaining in our time with monumental white marble mantelpieces made even more so by an imposing group of figures in pseudo-Grecian costume with a small insignificant clock dial or one of the overpowering gilt conceptions of the so-called 'Empire style'.

After running the gamut of the fanciful, 'Frenchy' styles, clock cases reverted to the 'stone age' and appeared as a simple dial set in a block of black marble. These, too, were highly popular as wedding gifts and presentations to club secretaries and others for 'faithful service'—in fact many of these 'horological mausoleums' still bear a brass plate inscribed with the recipient's name.

Changing days bring changing ways and in recent years the clocks which were the children of those nineteenth-century 'artists' whom one Victorian writer termed 'the emancipators of design' have mostly disappeared from the domestic scene. In the present century, the finer clock cases instead of being 'designed' are copied from those always satisfying styles produced

62. Modern reproduction of an early brass lantern clock fitted with lever escapement

63. Modern copy of a striking clock made by Bartholomew Newsam, c. 1580. The original is in the British Museum

during the golden age of furnishings two hundred years ago. Admittedly, other modern designs have been evolved by adapting elements of eighteenth-century originals, but the adaptations have generally retained the traditional simplicity even though in most instances they bear slight resemblance to the 'adaptee'.

While, in clockmaking as in other crafts, the handicraft of man has been largely replaced by the machine, excellent copies of the clocks of long-ago are being produced by present-day makers. Most of these, admittedly, have a modern eight-day lever move-ment and, to meet present-day requirements, there are minor variations. For example, a minute hand is added to copies of those early models which had only one hand. This addition is made with the reproductions of the table and brass lantern clocks (62), but such a variation from the original is a concession to our unfamiliarity with clock dials fitted with only one hand rather than an attempt by the modern clockmaker to introduce one of those superfluous 'improvements' so often found with reproductions of early designs.

With some of the copies, it is possible to point to certain minor omissions, such as with the modern reproduction of the clock by Bartholomew Newsam. Reference has been made previously to this clock in Chapter Seven and if the description given there is compared with the details of the copy in (63), it will be noticed that the small hinged door on each side is omitted. This was not an oversight on the part of the modern maker, but a matter of economy in the cost, for he realized that with the present-day movement the doors are unnecessary. Other differences which are noticeable are the addition of a minute hand and the increase of two inches in the height of the reproduction.

Another small clock to be successfully copied was made by the slightly later Edmund Bull who worked in Fleet Street three hundred years ago. It is similar to the one by Newsam, but instead of the perforated dome and ornament, the top is of four sections of quarter round joined to form a domical outline which was adopted later with bracket clocks (see Chapter Eight). Reproductions of table clocks with horizontal dials are also made and we illustrate (64) an example from an original by Andreas Fehmel who was working during the late seventeenth century.

Like those of other early dials, the numerals on the dial of the Fehmel clock are apt, at first sight, to be confusing. The hour ring is engraved I to XII in roman numerals and another ring inside it is engraved with the numbers 13 to 24 in arabic figures; the outside edge of the hour ring is divided into minutes and the square frame of the dial engraved in roman numerals, I, II, III, IIII. In this way, the dial shows the twenty-four hours of the day, i.e., the first twelve being indicated by roman figures and the following twelve by arabic; the roman figures on the frame marking the quarter hours, the I being placed above III o'clock, the II above VI, the III above IX and the IIII above XII.

Where, as in the case of lantern clocks, the dial of the original shows only the quarter-hour divisions with a fleur-de-lis or other device to mark the half-hour, there are, as it were, two schools

64.   Square table clock copied from an original made by Andreas Fehmel about 1680.   The first twelve hours of the day are shown on the horizontal dial in roman and the second twelve in an inner circle in arabic numerals

among modern makers.   One school engraves the inner circle with the original forty-eight divisions or quarter-hours, but the other utilizes the circle for the more familiar sixty minutes of the hour.   We will concede the latter to be more convenient, but it takes something from the reproduction clock.

One well-known house which handles clocks of both the past and the present adopted the slogan 'Back to the Old Masters' in describing the modern copies.   On the desk as this is being written there are a number of illustrations of examples made by present-day craftsmen who have gone back to the old masters.   Bracket, grandfather and even sedan clocks are all represented including one in a walnut case with a pierced and chased brass basket-top copied from an original clock by Jonathan Lowndes who was working in Pall Mall during the reign of William and Mary. Others were copied from clocks by Edward East, Thomas Tompion, Joseph Knibb and similarly famous English makers.

We have said that modern reproductions of early clocks are mostly fitted with what is generally spoken of as the lever movement. The lever escapement was invented in about 1760 by Thomas Mudge who made a watch with this escapement for Queen Charlotte, the wife of George III. But while it proved satisfactory, the invention was not generally adopted until about

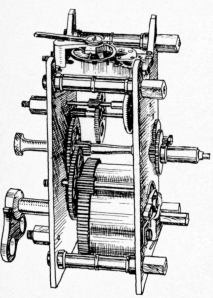
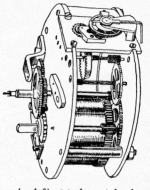

65. (*on left*) Modern eight-day movement illustrating how the drive of the spring is transmitted from the great wheel through the various pinions and wheels to the escapement

66. (*above*) Small eight-day movement with lever escapement. Compare with 13

a century later. The advantage of the lever escapement is that it allows a clock movement to be compact and therefore suitable for quite small clocks, yet the general principle of the mechanism is similar to that of the fusee and spring.

This will be seen by comparing the fusee and spring movement with the verge escapement (13) and those with the lever escapement (65, 66). The spring in the barrel of (13), as explained in Chapter Five, pulls the cat-gut line from the fusee on to the barrel and in so doing turns the fusee which thus furnishes the driving force. With the present-day movement (65, 66) the driving force is direct from the spring in the barrel to which the driving wheel is fixed. And by studying the illustrations it is possible in each movement to follow the transmission of the power and the gearing through the various pinions and wheels to the escapement.

Radical changes with clocks resulted from two inventions each made by the son of a clergyman—Robert Hooke who gave us the anchor escapement and Thomas Mudge, the lever escapement. The former allowed clocks with long pendulums to be fitted to wood cases of bracket clocks and the latter resulted in a movement without a pendulum which allows the present-day clockmaker to produce a movement for the miniature bracket clock cases copied from the seventeenth and eighteenth century originals (see 67, 68).

These charming little timepieces as well as the full sized copies of early bracket clocks prove conclusively that, given the time and the encouragement, the modern craftsman can and does produce work equal to that which has come down from bygone generations. Unfortunately the group of men responsible for these modern cases is all too small; moreover, each one is a specialist who, dependent upon and proud of his own handicraft, produces only a limited number.

No style of early case is beyond their powers to reproduce whether it be one of the seventeenth-century basket-top or one of the several styles that followed. As a general rule, the modern cases are of finely figured walnut, each section being made and assembled by hand, the original being followed with the same faithfulness as a woman follows one of those mysterious paper patterns of some garment. In rare instances, the case of a miniature bracket clock will be made of onyx, one of which is illustrated in (69); this has the gilt basket-top fashionable during the late seventeenth century.

In recognizing the skill of the modern case maker we must not overlook that of the metal worker, the dial maker and the man

67.   Modern bracket clock
with lever movement in a
walnut basket-top case. The
divisions of the dial, the
hands and corner orna-
ments repeat the early forms

68.   Modern reproduction of an
eighteenth-century bracket clock
with an arch dial in walnut case

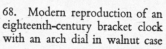

who fashions the hands. The pierced brass basket-tops, the corner pieces and similar ornaments in the arch of a dial and the handles are cast from copies of original clocks. Both the early and simpler cherub head with wings and the later more intricate corner ornaments, such as the mask and scrolls (see 59), are used with reproduction clocks and the manner in which these are tooled and finished is a further tribute to present-day craftsmen.

Obviously, a copy of an early clock is achieved by assembling the products of individual craftsmen in the same way as the original was assembled. The dials for instance have a similar silvered hour ring with matted centre, the quarter divisions on the inside and, on the outer edge, the minute divisions with the arabic figures over the roman hour numeral. The same applies to the hands of the clocks, for the delicate and intricate pierced work of the various designs must of necessity call for highly skilled handicraft.

Most of the present-day copies of the old-time grandfather and the full sized bracket clocks are fitted with a striking or a chiming train. We are illustrating the movement of a modern clock (70) which strikes the half-hours to allow comparison with that of the grandfather clock shown in Figure 9. While there are noticeable differences, it will be seen that the modern clock retains the old-time snail, the rack and the lifting piece. The modern movement, however, has one valuable feature which is absent in the older clocks—the hands may be moved backward or forward without damaging the mechanism.

Though, to-day, we have reliable watches, the tradition of the portable clock persists in what are still known as carriage clocks. And the small timepieces in gilt-metal cases fitted with a handle at the top and enclosed in a leather case for travelling are in fairly common use. Some of the modern carriage clocks strike the hours and half-hours while others have an alarm which can be set to 'arouse the traveller'. Occasionally, you may come on one with a repeating movement, but these are usually by some earlier French clockmaker. The writer happened upon one some years ago in an auction room where it was part of a lot of several clocks. It needed repairing and this was an intricate and somewhat

costly job; but it proved the truth of the slogan, 'The pleasure is
enjoyed long after the cost is forgotten' for it is a real pleasure to
press the little knob in the dark and hear the chimes sound the
last hour and quarter.

In addition to the reproductions of traditional designs, the

69. Miniature bracket
clock with modern lever
movement in an onyx case
with pierced gilt metal
basket top.   H. 6½ in.

variety of modern cases both short and tall is legion.   In an earlier
chapter we mentioned the seventeenth-century writer John
Smith's reference to a long case clock as 'the coffin'.   While this
description might apply to certain quite early long case clocks, it
assuredly does to some made at the present time.   In fact the
'design' of these severe box-like forms might well have been
inspired by an Egyptian mummy-case—minus the hieroglyphics.

Later technicians have succeeded where those of other days
failed, for they have given us clocks that need no winding.   Old-
style lantern and dials in cases copied from early bracket clocks

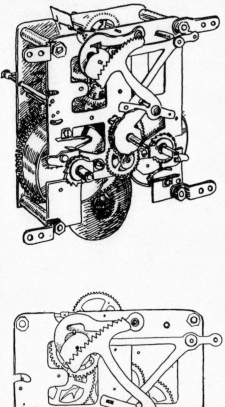

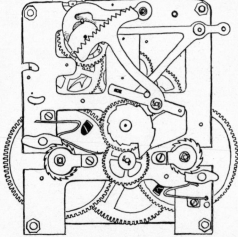

70.   Modern half-hour striking movement.   The upper drawing
shows the winding barrel of the striking train, the later counter-
part of the spring and fusee (compare 13) and the fan-fly which
regulates the speed of the striking train.   Comparison of the
lower drawing with that of the early clock (9) shows the snail,
the rack and lifting piece are still retained

and in cases of modern vintage are now operated by electricity; but efficient as this may be, a clock nonetheless needs a constant supply of power to record the time, consequently with the intermittent 'load-shedding' an electric clock is apt to be a source of irritation.   And once again we are brought to acknowledge that handwork is more to be relied upon than the machine—a clock wound by hand will at least continue to tell the time and strike the hours provided the movement is in good order.

SECTION 7
Through Three Centuries

CHAPTER SIXTEEN

FREEMAN CLOCKMAKERS

CLOCKMAKING AS ONE of the established trades in this country may be said to date from about the end of the sixteenth century when English clockmakers began to make domestic timepieces of the lantern type. The craft was then more or less allied with the blacksmiths and there are indications that it was regulated to an extent by the Blacksmiths' Company which was incorporated in 1578 as the Blacksmiths and Spurriers. With the development and expansion of their trade and the increase in the number of craftsmen who came from France, the English clockmakers decided that their interests could be better safeguarded if they themselves were incorporated and thus attain the status of an official gild or company.

In 1630, therefore, a group of the more prominent men subscribed funds for the necessary expenses and petitioned Charles I for a charter; this was granted in the following year and what is known as the Worshipful Company of Clockmakers came into being. The former close association between the clockmakers and the blacksmiths is seen in the fact that a number of the original petitioners for the charter were freemen of the Blacksmiths' Company and a larger number of freemen of that (and some of the other older City companies) were admitted as brothers of the Clockmakers' Company; in fact, one, Robert Grinkin, was master of the Blacksmiths in 1609 and forty years later was elected master of the Clockmakers.

Like other trade gilds, the Clockmakers, by their charter, were given wide powers to regulate and control the craft and to protect the public from 'bad, deceitful or insufficient clocks, watches, larums, sundials, boxes and cases'—the word 'insufficient' being used in its now almost forgotten meaning of lacking quality. To this end, the Company had the right of search and seizure, a right they exercised rigidly until the time of George II. In addition, they were authorized to make and enforce by-laws governing clockmakers in and within a radius of ten miles of the City of London and to generally control the craft and trade throughout the country.

Their regulations applying to apprentices were particularly strict and the Company saw to it that these were observed. Here, it may be of interest to repeat part of the original regulation which is quoted in full by Mr. W. S. Pennefather in his preface to that valuable reference, the *Register of Apprentices* of the Company of Clockmakers, compiled in 1931 by Mr. Charles Edward Atkins:

Item, it is ordained, that every apprentice having truly served his apprenticeship, and being admitted a Freeman of the said Society, shall, according to the custom of other Companies, serve his Master, or some other of the same Fellowship, by the space of two years as journeyman; and, at the end of the same two years, it shall be, by virtue hereof, lawful for the Master or Warden, or Wardens, of the said Fellowship, to call any person or persons whatsoever, being a member or professor of the same trade, before he or they be admitted, or allowed of, to be a lawful master, to bring in his or their masterpiece or masterpieces, which he or they shall be appointed to make by the Master, Wardens, and Assistants, or the major part of them (whereof the Master and one of the Wardens to be two), what piece, or what manner of whole or intire piece, he shall make, and where he shall make it, which, being by the Master, Wardens, and Assistants, of the said Company or Fellowship, or the more part of them, allowed and approved of he shall, from thenceforth, be admitted a work-master of the said Society, and not before; for which said admittance he shall pay to the use of the said Master, Wardens, and Fellowship, the sum of twenty shillings, and to the clerk three shillings four pence, and to the beadle twelve-pence.

This regulation continues with the prolixity and abundance of commas typical of the period at which it was written and equally typical of what to-day is known as 'Whitehallese' or 'legalese'. Expressed in the form our American friends term 'shirt-sleeve English', it orders that an apprentice had to serve a term of, usually seven, years and having completed his time could be 'admitted and sworn a free clockmaker'; but he had to spend a further two years as a journeyman in the shop of an established clockmaker, at the end of which time he must make a piece of work ordered by the Master and Wardens of the Company, to whom it had to be submitted. This job of work was known as the aspiring clockmaker's 'masterpiece' because, if approved, it allowed him to become a 'master clockmaker' or in modern language, 'his own boss'.

Upward of sixty women appear in the Register of Apprentices and of these sixteen were apprenticed during the last quarter of the seventeenth century, the earliest being Mary Clark and Ruth Smith in 1674. Only eight of these women became 'freemen' however, the others, after serving their time, doubtless working as journeymen in various shops where, it is probable, they were employed more particularly in the making of watches.

One or two interesting facts come to light from the entries relating to these women: Nineteen were indentured to women 'masters', the most prominent of whom was Elinor Moseley who was admitted as a 'freeman' in 1726 and who, at different times during the first half of the eighteenth century, was responsible for teaching the craft to seven young women.

Where a woman was apprenticed to a man, it was customary also to name his wife in the indenture; thus Elinor Moseley herself was apprenticed to 'George Tyler and Lucy his wife', though Lucy was not actively engaged in clockmaking. Again, a daughter would be apprenticed to a clockmaker-father as was the case with Anne, Mary and Sarah Webster, each of whom was apprenticed during the later seventeenth century to their father, Robert Webster, the founder of this well-known family of clock-makers of whom succeeding generations have been prominent in the craft since the reign of Charles II to the present time.

In compiling the following list, the writer would express his gratitude to the Worshipful Company of Clockmakers for permission to examine their registers; and he is and will remain specially sensible of the unfailing kindness of Mr. Raymond Smith, the Librarian of the Guildhall Library, and the staff at that 'peaceful oasis'.

Regarding the dates: That given immediately after the name of each freeman denotes the year in which he was admitted 'a free clockmaker', 'a brother of the Company' or elected to the Livery. In some few instances, the date is preceded by the abbreviation '*c.*' (*circa*, about) suggesting that the man was working as a clockmaker before that date and was one of the early members of the Company. A date preceded by 'M.' indicates that the man became Master of the Company and the year or years he was elected to that office. For example, the entry 'John Thwaites, 1782. M. 1815, 1819 and 1820', signifies that this man was admitted a Freeman in 1782 and elected Master in each of the three years, 1815, 1819 and 1820.

A LIST OF CLOCKMAKERS

A LIST OF CLOCKMAKERS

WITH a view to making the list more convenient and easier as a reference, the surnames of the clockmakers have been arranged alphabetically; the chronological order has, in consequence, been disregarded except in the relatively few instances of men having both the same surname and Christian names. Where a difference occurs in the spelling of a surname, the variation is noted.

ABBOTT
John, 1788.
Joseph, 1873. M. 1899.
Peter, 1719.
Philip, 1704.
Thomas, 1740.
William, 1774.
ACAM, Robert, 1774.
ACHURCH, William, 1699.
ACOTT, William, 1791.
ACTON
Abraham, 1710.
Abraham, 1738.
John, 1677.
Thomas, 1677.
ADAMS
Francis Bryant, 1802.
Francis Bryant, 1828.
M. 1848, 1849, and 1865.
Francis Bryant, M. 1914 and 1922.
George, 1752.
George William, 1829. M. 1861 and 1868.
Herbert Jordan, M. 1886 and 1897.
James, 1832. M. 1854 and 1857.
James Scovell, 1858. M. 1876, 1882, 1907 and 1917.
John, 1766.
John, 1772.
ADAMSON
John, 1686.
John, 1813.
ADDIS
George Curzon, 1787.
William, 1745. M. 1764.
ADDISON, John Garratt Curtis, M. 1866 and 1871.
ADEANE
Henry, 1675.
Henry, 1706.
ADKINS, Thomas, 1745.
ADLINGTON, John, 1806.
ADNEY, Thomas, 1767.
AICKEN or **AICKIN**, George, 1777.
AINGE, Alexander, 1766.
ALBERT, Isaac, 1732.
ALCOCK, Thomas, c. 1630.
One of the petitioners

for incorporation of Company of Clock-makers.
ALDERMAN, Edwin, 1822.
ALDERSON, Josiah, 1758.
ALDRED, Leonard, 1671.
ALDRIDGE
John, 1725.
Thomas, 1769.
ALDWORTH, Samuel, 1697.
ALLAM
Andrew, 1664.
Robert, 1742.
ALLAWAY, John, 1695.
ALLEN
Charles, 1763.
Charles, 1770.
Elias, M. 1636.
George, 1771.
George, 1781.
James, 1635.
John, 1720.
John, 1753.
Joseph, 1781.
Nathaniel, 1662.
William, 1745.
ALLETT, George, 1691.
ALLING, Richard, 1722.
ALSOPE or **ALLSOP**, Joshua, 1689.
ALLSOPP, John, 1794.
ALMOND
John, 1671.
Ralph, 1646. M. 1678.
William, 1633.
ALVEY or **ALLVEY**
Henry Quiat, 1784.
Samuel, 1757.
Thomas, 1804.
AMBROSE
David, 1669.
Edward, 1637.
AMES
Richard, 1656. M. 1682.
William, 1682.
ANDERSON
Hugh, 1745.
John, 1776.
Samuel Thornton, 1801.
ANDERTON, William, 1818.
ANDREWS or **ANDREWES**
Benjamin, 1741.
James, 1719.
John, 1688.
Nathaniel, James, 1772.

Richard, 1703.
Robert, 1710.
Thomas, 1705.
William, 1719.
William, 1767.
ANNESS
William, 1796.
William, 1828.
ANSELL
George, 1776.
John, 1843.
Richard, 1680.
ANTRAM, Joseph, 1706.
APPLEBY
John James, 1823.
Joshua, 1719. M. 1745.
APPLEGARTH
Thomas, 1674.
APPLEY, Edmund, 1677.
ARCHER
Edward, 1712.
Henry, 1632.
John, 1660.
Richard Sewell, 1758.
Thomas, 1815.
William, 1843.
ARIELL
James, 1792.
Samuel, 1822.
ARIS, John, 1764.
ARLANDI, John, 1682.
ARMINGER, Joseph, 1688.
ARMSTRONG, John, 1724.
ARNOLD
Charles Willson, 1824.
John, 1783.
John Roger, 1796. M. 1817.
Thomas, 1703.
Thomas, 1750.
ARNOTT, Richard, 1808.
ARTHUR, William, 1676.
ASH
Ralph, 1646.
Robert, 1820.
Robert Francis, 1864.
ASHBY, Joseph, 1674.
ASHDOWN, Charles, 1833.
ASHFORD, Richard Henry, 1827.
ASHLEY, James, 1763.
ASHURST, William, 1699.
ASHWELL, Nicholas, 1649.
ASKE, Henry, 1676.
ASKEY, Thomas, 1832.

ASPINWALL or ASPINALL,
  Josiah, 1675.
ASSELIN, Francis, 1687.
ATCHISON, Robert, 1760.
ATKINS
  Charles Edward, M.
    1896, 1908 and 1927.
  Francis, 1759. M. 1780.
  George, 1788. M. 1845.
  George William, 1870.
    M. 1902 and 1916.
  Samuel Elliott, 1831.
    M. 1881 and 1889.
ATKINSON
  James, 1667.
  Thomas Benjamin, 1829.
ATLEE, Henry, 1672.
ATWILL, Walter Edward,
  1912.
AUSTEN, John, 1712.
AUSTIN
  Richard, 1769.
  Richard, 1817.
AVELINE, Daniel, 1731. M.
  1771.
AVENEL or AVENALL
  Edward, 1706.
  John, 1735.
AVERY
  Andrew, 1777.
  Joseph, 1811.
  Phillip, 1802.
AYMES, Richard, 1656.
AYRES, Richard, 1680.

BACON
  Charles, 1719.
  John, 1639.
  Thomas, 1791.
BACQUETT, Davyd, 1632.
BADDELEY, Phineas, 1661.
BADGER, John, 1720.
BAGLEY
  Thomas, 1658.
  Thomas, 1664.
BAGNALL or BAGNELL
  Henry, 1795.
  John, 1826.
  William, 1719.
  William Henry, 1839.
BAGSHAW
  Edward, 1691.
  William, 1722.
BAILEY or BAILY
  Edward Branston, 1738.
  James, 1761.
  Jeremiah, 1724.
  John, 1771.
BAKER
  Henry, 1781.
  John, 1781.
  John, 1813.
  Pointer, 1758.
  Richard, 1685.
  Richard, 1727.
  William, 1779.
BAKEWELL, Thomas, 1654.

BALDWIN or BALDWYN
  Henry Smith, 1785.
  Thomas, 1685.
  Thomas, 1706.
BALE
  Thomas, 1704.
BALFOUR, Joseph, 1761.
BALL
  John, 1637.
  Thomas, 1724.
BALLARD
  John, 1768.
  William, 1736.
BANBURY, John, 1685.
BANFIELD, Thomas, 1773.
BANGER, Edward, 1695.
BANKES, William, 1698.
BANKS, Robert, 1750.
BANNISTER or BANISTER
  Anthony, 1715.
  James, 1818.
  William, 1734.
BANTING, William, 1646.
BARACHIN, Stephen, 1687.
BARBER
  Charles, 1796.
  Jonas, 1682.
BARCLAY, John, 1787.
BARCOLE, John, 1647.
BARJON, John, 1685.
BARKER
  John, 1813.
  William, 1632.
BARKLEY, Samuel, 1722.
BARLOW, Thomas, 1692.
BARNARD,
  John, 1682.
  Robert, 1740.
BARNARDISTON,   John,
  1714.
BARNETT, John, 1682.
BARNSDALE
  Alfred John, 1885.
  Arthur, 1897.
  Charles, 1896.
  Frederick, 1895.
  Henry, 1888.
  Stanley, 1916.
  William, 1877. M. 1905.
  William James, 1885.
    M. 1918 and 1929.
BARNWELL, Richard, 1705.
BARRAUD or BARAUD
  Frederick, Joseph, 1806.
  Frederick Philip, 1838.
  Henry, 1633.
  Hilton Paul, 1846.
  James, 1815.
  John, 1813.
  Paul Philip, 1796. M.
    1810 and 1811.
BARRETT or BARRATT
  Henry, 1692.
  Henry, 1802.
  Samuel, 1701.
  Simon, 1678.
BARROW
  John, 1681. M. 1714.

  John, 1704.
  Nathaniel, 1660. M.
    1689.
  Samuel, 1696.
  William, 1710.
BARTHOLOMEW,   John
  1675.
BARTINGDALE,   Samuel
  William, 1870.
BARTON
  Mathias, 1804.
  Samuel, 1640.
BARTRAM or BERTRAM
  Symon, c. 1630. One of
    petitioners for incor-
    poration of Company
    of Clockmakers. M.
    1650 and 1651.
  William, 1684. M. 1732.
BARUGH, William, 1716.
BARWICK, James, 1798.
BASIRE, John, 1756.
BASKERVILLE
  Richard, 1749.
  Thomas, 1738.
BASS, George, 1722.
BATEMAN
  Andrew, 1786.
  Nathaniel, 1747.
BATES
  Joseph, 1687.
  Thomas, 1684.
BATGER, John, 1720.
BATHE, Thomas, 1757.
BATTEN or BATTIN, John,
  1668.
BATTERSON
  Henry, 1701.
  Robert, 1693.
BATTIN, Thomas, 1661.
BAXTER, Charles, 1681.
BAYES
  Benjamin, 1675.
  John, 1646.
BAYLEY or BAYLY (see
    BAILEY)
  Barnard, 1784.
  Edward, 1658.
  James, 1761.
  James, 1768.
  Jeffrey, 1646. M. 1674
    and 1675.
  John, 1700.
  John, 1708.
  Josiah, 1778.
  Thomas, 1786.
  William, 1663.
BEAKE
  John Covell, 1752.
  Jonathan, 1724.
BEARCROFT, Samuel, 1808.
BEARD (see BOAD)
BEASLEY or BEESLEY
  Ann, 1769.
  John, 1719.
  Nathaniel, 1694.
  Thomas, 1683.
BEAUVAIS, Simon, 1690.

BECK or BECKE
Christopher, 1761.
John, 1681.
Nicholas, 1669.
Richard, 1653.
BECKMAN or BEECKMAN
Daniel, 1680.
Daniel, 1726.
John, 1695.
BECKNER, Abraham, 1652.
BEDELL, Joseph, 1684.
BEEG, Christiana, 1698.
BELCHER, Thomas, 1750.
BELL
Benjamin, 1657. M.
1682.
Boucher, 1772.
John, 1719.
Joseph, 1691.
William, 1815.
BELLARD, John, 1674.
BELLINGER
John, 1686.
John, 1725.
BENBRIDGE, Thomas, 1683.
BENJAMIN, Joel, 1832.
BENN
Anthony, 1742. M. 1763.
Robert, 1716.
Thomas, 1764.
Thomas, 1771.
William, 1786.
BENNETT
Charles, 1824.
George, 1704.
John, 1678.
John, 1712.
John, 1733.
John (Sir), 1871.
Mansell, 1688.
Richard, 1715.
Richard, 1813.
Samuel, 1716.
Samuel, 1742.
Thomas, 1720.
William, 1687.
William, 1692.
William, 1729.
BENSON
John, 1669.
Samuel, 1700.
BENTLEY, John, 1813.
BERAUD (see BARRAUD)
BERRINGTON or BARRING-
TON, Urian, 1684.
BERRY
John, 1688. M. 1723.
John, 1692.
John, 1697.
John, 1728.
Samuel, 1705.
BERTRAM (see BARTRAM),
William, 1684. M. 1732.
BEST, Robert, 1783.
BESTWICK, Henry, 1686.
BETHELL, William, 1770.
BETTS
Job, 1656.

Samuel, c. 1640.
BEVERELY, James, 1691.
BEYER, John, 1769.
BEZAR, Stephen, 1648.
BICKNELL, Francis, 1665.
BIDDLE, Joseph, 1684.
BIDLAKE or BIRDLAKE
James, 1779.
James Hodgson, 1809.
Thomas, 1809.
BILLINGHURST, Henry,
1757.
BILLINGTON, Robert, 1742.
BILLOP, William, 1688.
BIRCH
George, 1901.
Thomas, 1658.
Thomas, 1682.
William, 1840.
BIRCHALL, George, 1868.
BIRD
Luke, 1683.
Luke, 1740.
Michael, 1682.
Samuel Joseph, 1813.
Samuel Joseph Jr.,1829.
William, c. 1749.
BIRDWHISTELL or BIRD-
WHISSELL
Francis, 1687.
Isaac, 1692.
John, 1718.
Thomas, 1693.
BISHOP
Samuel, 1781.
Thomas, 1816.
BISSE or BYSSE, Edward,
1632.
BITTLESTON, John, 1781.
BLACKBOROW, James,
1711.
BLACKBOURNE or BLACK-
BOURN
Robert, 1720.
William, 1739.
BLACKBURN
William, 1768.
William, 1816.
BLACKETER, Peter, 1786.
BLACKETT, John, 1809.
BLACKWELL, William Ide,
1835.
BLINKO, John, 1819.
BLISS, Ambrose, 1653.
BLUNDELL
Richard, 1682.
William, 1716.
BLUNT, Edward, 1763.
BOAD or BEARD
Thomas, 1692.
Thomas, 1744.
BODDELL, Josiah, 1741.
BODDENHAM, Edward,
1719.
BODDINGTON, John, 1734.
BODILY or BODDILY, Eliz-
abeth, 1692.

BONNER
Charles, 1659.
Charles, 1705.
BONUS, Simon Peter, 1790.
BOOKER, Thomas, 1759.
BOONE, Edward, 1691.
BOOSEY
John, 1773.
Thomas, 1792.
BOOTH
James, 1778.
Richard, 1785.
Samuel, 1829.
William, 1790.
BOOTY, Alexander, 1776.
BOSCH, Ulrich, 1652.
BOSLEY
Charles, 1749.
Joseph, 1725.
BOUCHERET or BOUCHET,
Jacob, 1728.
BOULT, Joseph, 1709.
BOUQUET (see also BACK-
QUETT)
David, 1793.
Solomon, 1651.
Solomon, 1683.
BOUVET, George, 1739.
BOWEN
Francis, 1655.
John, 1709.
Richard, 1657.
Richard, 1678.
Thomas, 1796.
BOWLEY, Devereux, 1718.
M. 1759.
BOWMAN, James, 1743.
BOWTELL
Samuel, 1681.
William, 1704.
BOWYER, William, c. 1632.
BOYCE
James, 1692.
Matthias, 1863.
Thomas, 1695.
BOYLE, Richard, 1660.
BRACKLEY, George, 1677.
BRADFORD
Thomas, 1680.
Thomas, 1692.
Thomas, 1710.
BRADLEY
Benjamin, 1728.
Henry, 1681.
Langley, 1695. M. 1726.
Luke, 1726.
BRADSHAW
Edward, 1736.
Henry, 1696.
John, 1658.
John, 1731.
Richard, 1725.
BRAITHWAITE or BRATH-
WAITE, John, 1768.
BRANDON, Benjamin, 1689.
BRANDRETH, Joseph, 1718.
BRANT, Richard, 1700.
BRATTEL, John, 1761.

BRAY
John, 1733.
Robert, 1728.
BRAFIELD or BRAYFIELD
John, 1716.
Thomas, 1682.
Thomas, 1762.
William, 1678.
William, 1712.
BRAYLEY, Joseph, 1802.
BRAZIER, John, 1819.
BREACH, WILLIAM, 1773.
BREAMES, Leonard, 1633.
BREAN or BREAM, Casper, 1716.
BREESE
Edward, 1890.
James, 1888.
BRERETON, Henry William, 1791.
BREWER, John, 1677.
BREYNTON, Vaughan, 1693.
BRIANSON, Edward, 1768.
BRICKER, William, 1736.
BRIDGEMAN
Edward, 1662.
James, 1801.
BRIGDEN, Henry, 1682.
BRIDGER, Samuel, 1704.
BRIGGS
John, 1669.
Richard, 1756.
BRIGHTRIDGE, Henry William, 1790.
BRINKLEY, William, 1766.
BRITTAINE
Boaz, 1679.
Stephen, 1692.
Stephen, 1728.
BROAD
Thomas, 1682.
William, 1792.
BROADHEAD, Benjamin, 1709.
BROCKBANK
John, 1769.
John Edward, 1807.
Myles, 1776.
William, 1807.
BRODIE
Hugh, 1779.
Hugh, 1811.
BROMHALL, Woorsley,1735.
BROOK or BROOKE
Edmund, 1709.
Edward, 1872.
George, 1681.
John, 1632.
John Walter, 1803.
Richard, 1810.
Samuel, 1770.
BROOKES or BROOKS
Charles, 1824.
Edward, 1690.
John, 1773.
John, 1777.
Samuel, 1798.
Samuel Augustus, 1867.

Thomas, 1738.
Thomas, 1766.
Thomas, 1787.
Thomas, 1823.
William, 1754.
William, 1760.
William, 1787.
BROOME, Thomas, 1652.
BROUGH, Samuel, 1792.
BROWN or BROWNE
George, 1773.
Henry, 1825.
Henton, 1726. M. 1753.
James, 1687.
James, 1766. M. 1770.
James, 1767.
John, 1652. M. 1681.
John, 1773.
John, 1786.
John, 1807.
Matthew, 1633.
Philip, 1688.
Renock, 1773.
Richard, 1675.
Robert, 1768.
Robert, 1771.
Thomas, 1676.
Thomas, 1703.
Thomas, 1747.
William, 1719.
William, 1801.
BRUNWIN, Henry, 1775.
BRUTON, Thomas, 1778.
BRYAN
John, 1773.
Richard, 1696.
Samuel, 1765.
William, 1772.
BRYANT, Thomas, 1773.
BUARDSELL, William, 1771.
BUCK
Edward, 1632.
Richard, 1726.
BUCKENHILL
Edward, 1687.
John, 1672.
BUCKLEE, David, 1785.
BUCKNER, Philip, 1667.
BUCKNEY
Charles, 1908.
Frank, 1908.
BUCQUET (see BOUQUET),
David Alexander,1793.
BULKLEY or BULKELEY,
Thomas, 1715.
BULL
John, 1632.
William, 1842.
BULLBY, John, 1632.
BULLOCK, Thomas Adolphus, M. 1919 and 1920.
BULTE or BULTY, Daniel, 1663.
BUMSTEAD, Robert, 1707.
BUNCE
James, 1721.
Matthew, 1698.
BUNTING, William, 1645.

BURCH, William, 1840.
BURCHETT or BURCHET
John, 1731.
John, 1751.
Philip, 1715.
BURDETT, Henry, 1734.
BURDITT, Joseph, 1805.
BURGESS or BURGES
Elias, 1681.
George, 1780.
William, 1770.
BURGIS, John, 1632.
BURNETT, Richard, 1705.
BURRELL, Boys Err, 1796.
BURROWS
Joseph, 1773.
William James, 1772.
BURSON, George, 1749.
BURTON
Abraham, 1657.
John, 1776.
William, 1770.
BUSCHMANN or BUSHMAN
John, 1692.
John Baptist, 1725.
John Baptist William, 1774.
Joseph, 1759.
BUSH
James, 1729.
Walter, 1770.
BUTCHER
Benjamin, 1781.
Benjamin Henry, 1813.
Gersham, 1749.
Henry, 1760.
Henry Charles, 1818.
William, 1815.
BUTLER, John, 1724.
BUXTON, Wilson, 1733.
BYFORD, William, 1815.
BYWORTH
George, 1815.
Thomas, 1815.

CABRIER
Charles, 1697.
Charles, 1726. M. 1757.
Charles, 1756.
John, 1730.
CADE, Simon, 1688.
CALCOTT, Tobias, 1664.
CALDERWOOD, Thomas, 1724.
CALLEY, Joseph, 1752.
CALLIBER (see COLLIBER)
CALLIS, Robert, 1764.
CAM, William, 1686.
CAMBRIDGE, Samuel, 1698.
CAMDEN
William, 1708.
William, 1751.
CANCHE, James, 1692.
CANN, John, 1649.
CANNANS, John, 1723.
CARD, Edmund, 1679.

CAREY or CARY
George, 1679.
Thomas, 1706.
CARPENTER
Thomas, 1767.
William, 1781.
CARRINGTON or CHARRING-
TON
George, 1782.
Harry Charles, 1791.
James, 1717.
Richard, 1759.
Robert, 1743.
Samuel, M. 1768.
Thomas, 1748.
CARRUTHERS, George, 1773.
CARSTENS, John, 1707.
CARSWELL, John, 1819.
CARTE, John, 1695.
CARTER
Edmund, 1740.
Edmund, 1749.
John, 1728.
John, 1829. M. 1856,
1859 and 1864.
John William, 1870. M.
1898 and 1912.
Joyce, 1776.
Leon, Augustus, 1725.
Robert, 1731.
Thomas, 1659.
Thomas, 1699.
CARTWRIGHT
George, 1706.
William, 1714.
CARVER, Isaac, 1687.
CASS, George, 1771.
CASTENS, John, 1707.
CASTER, William, 1697.
CASTERTON, James, 1803.
CATCHPOOL, William, 1826.
CATLEY, Daniel, 1731.
CATON
Francis, 1827.
Gilbert, 1747.
CATTELL
Thomas, 1688.
William, 1672.
CAVENDISH, Richard, 1808.
CAWDRON, George, 1684.
CAWDWELL, Thomas, 1742.
CAWLEY, William, 1775.
CAWNE or CAWE, Robert,
1675.
CESAR or CAESAR, Daniel,
1703.
CEXT, Catherine, 1730.
CHADWICK, Joseph, 1815.
CHALK or CHALKE, James,
1796.
CHALLAND, William, 1749.
CHAMBERLAIN or CHAM-
BERLAYNE
Nathaniel, 1685. M.
1717.
Nathaniel, 1659.
Thomas, 1687.
CHAMBERS, Robert, 1720.

CHAMPION
John, 1640.
John, 1651.
CHANCELLOR, John, 1788.
CHANDLER, Edward, 1724.
CHAPMAN
Peter, 1737.
Richard, 1770.
Simon, 1675.
Thomas, 1790.
CHAPPELLE, Robert, 1720.
CHARAS, Charles Samson,
1692.
CHARIE, Dennis Lewis,
1829.
CHARLSTROM, William,
1802.
CHARLETON
Matjonah, 1729.
John, M. 1640. One of
petitioners for incor-
poration of Company
of Clockmakers.
CHARRINGTON, Samuel (see
CARRINGTON)
CHATER
Eliezer, 1751. M. 1772.
James, 1726.
James, 1753.
John, 1766.
Nathaniel, 1782.
Richard, 1781.
CHAUVELL, James, 1699.
CHEESEMAN, Daniel, 1699.
CHELTENHAM, Michael,
1712.
CHENEY, Withers, 1657.
CHERRINGTON, John Stan-
ley, 1814.
CHILCOTT
Richard, 1690.
John, 1721.
CHILD
Henry, 1641. M. 1664.
Henry, 1677.
John, 1769.
Ralph, 1661.
Richard, 1632.
CHILTON, Thomas, 1738.
CHISMAN
George, 1772.
Timothy, 1779. M. 1803.
CHOTARD, Paul, 1742.
CHRISTIE
William, 1843.
William, Henry Maho-
ney (Sir), M. 1901 and
1913.
CHURCHMAN, Michael, 1694.
CLANFIELD, Henry, 1707.
CLARIDGE, Robert, 1802.
CLARK or CLARKE
Cureton, 1747.
Daniel, 1868. M. 1891.
George, 1632.
George, 1787.
George, 1803.

Henry, 1812.
Humphrey, 1668.
James, 1768.
John, 1691.
John, 1725.
John, 1770.
John, 1788.
John Stanford, 1696.
Randell, 1778.
Richard, 1720.
Richard, 1790.
Robert Cowell, 1774.
Thomas, 1709.
Thomas, 1720.
William, 1654.
William Richard, 1803.
CLARKSON, John, 1657.
CLAXTON
Richard, 1646.
Thomas, 1646. M. 1670.
CLAY
Samuel, 1687.
William, 1652.
CLAYTON, Caleb, 1734.
CLEETER, William, 1709.
CLEMENT or CLEMENTS
Edward, 1671.
Robert, 1686.
William, 1677. M. 1694.
CLEMSON or CLEMPSON
Richard, 1673.
CLERKE
George, 1782.
George, 1802.
Nathaniel, 1782.
CLEVELAND, Henry, 1799.
CLIFTON
Thomas, 1651.
Thomas, 1687.
CLIVERDON
Richard, 1762.
Thomas, 1722.
CLOSON, Peter, 1636.
CLOWES or CLEWES
James, 1671.
John, 1672.
Ralph, 1703.
CLUER, Obadiah, 1709.
CLUTER, William, 1709.
CLYATT
Abraham, 1680.
John, 1708.
Lemuel, 1712.
Samuel, 1672.
William, 1709.
COATS or COATES
James, 1788.
John Hardwick, 1822.
COBB, John, 1703.
COBBETT, George, 1810.
COBHAM
James, 1739.
John, 1737.
Stockley, 1737.
COCK, Charles, 1736.
COLAMBELL,   Anthony
1776.

150

COLE
Aquila, 1780.
Benjamin, 1733.
Daniel, 1726.
Edward, 1721.
John, 1729.
Richard, 1822.
COLEMAN or COLMAN
John, 1781.
Thomas, 1806.
COLES
Abraham, 1775.
James, 1761.
COLLEY
John, 1749.
Joseph, 1752 (see CAL-
LEY)
COLLIBER
John, 1703.
Thomas, 1726.
COLLIER or COLLYER
Benjamin, 1693.
John, 1777.
Marshall, 1818.
Robert, 1738.
COLLINGRIDGE, Edmund,
1800.
COLLINGWOOD
Samuel, 1759.
Thomas, 1734.
COLLINS
Clement, 1705.
John, 1701.
John, 1726.
Peter, 1687.
Richard Barret, 1751.
COLSON or COLSTON
John, 1646.
John, 1653.
Richard, 1682.
COMFORT, William, 1646.
COMMANDER, Joseph, 1841.
COMPORT
Ebenezer, 1728.
Joseph, 1767.
COMPTON, Adam, 1716.
CONDY, Thomas, 1692.
CONNELL, William, 1846.
CONNIGERVITS, William,
1811.
CONNY, John, 1640.
CONSTANTINE, John, 1716.
CONYERS
Richard, 1689.
Richard, 1716.
COOK or COOKE
Job, 1750.
John, 1649.
John, 1662.
John, 1713.
John, 1775.
John, 1785.
Joseph, 1715.
Richard, 1776.
Robert, 1667.
Robert, 1804.
Thomas, 1699.

William, 1681.
William George, 1916.
COOMBES or COOMBS
Fisher, 1728.
James, 1719.
John, 1779.
Joseph, 1720.
COOPER
Hugh, 1653.
John, 1813.
Thomas, 1798.
Thomas, 1894.
COPE, Peter, 1638.
COPELAND, Alexander,
1809.
CORDON, Richard, 1729.
CORDREY or CORDEROY
Philip, 1679.
Thomas, 1670.
CORKE, William Richard,
M. 1923.
CORNISH, Michael, 1661.
COSBEY or COSBY, Robert,
1653.
COSTER
Robert, 1655.
Thomas, 1764.
William, 1660.
COTHER, William, 1668.
COTSWORTH, John, 1669.
COTTEREL or COTTRILL
John, 1721.
William, 1694.
COTTON
John, 1695.
John, 1719.
Richard, 1819.
COTTONBELT, John, 1729.
COUCHE, Charles, 1727.
COULSON
Robert, 1791.
William, 1814.
COURTAULD, Augustine,
1748.
COURTNEY, John, 1768.
COVENTRY, Carr, 1657.
COWARD, William, 1681.
COWDEROY, William, 1820.
COWELL
John, 1759.
John Flower, 1735.
COWPE
Edward, 1687.
James, 1654.
COX
Benjamin, 1733.
Henry, 1826.
John, 1878.
Thomas, 1708.
COXETER or COXITER
John, 1646. M. 1661 and
1662.
Nicholas, 1646. M. 1671
and 1677.
Thomas, 1673.
William, 1654.
CRAGG
John, 1788.

John, 1856.
Richard, 1660.
CRAIGHEAD, William Liv-
ingstone, 1847.
CRAVEN, Thomas, 1688.
CRAWLY
Thomas, 1660.
William, 1756.
CRAYFORD or CRAFFORD,
Francis, 1718.
CRAYLE, Richard, c. 1630.
One of the petitioners
for the incorporation of
the Company of Clock-
makers.
CREED or CREEDE
John, 1728.
Robert, 1699.
Robert, 1733.
Thomas, 1668.
Thomas, 1674.
CRIPPLE
William, 1702.
William, 1750.
CRISP, John, 1770.
CROCKER, James, 1716.
CROCKFORD
Matthew, 1658.
Matthew, 1693.
CROFT
John, 1665.
William, 1829.
CROLL, Alexander Angus
(Col.), M. 1877 and
1884.
CROMPTON
Adam, 1716.
Wilkinson, 1756.
CRONIN
Harry Stowell (Rev.),
M. 1915.
Walter Daniel, M. 1900.
CROOK or CROOKE
Benjamin, 1784.
Joseph, 1770.
Peter, 1724.
Sampson, 1668.
CROSS, John, 1831.
CROSSFIELD, John, 1794.
CROSSLANDS
James, 1818.
John Haywood, 1785.
CROUCH
Edward, 1691. M. 1719.
George, 1668.
Robert, 1722.
CROUCHER, Joseph, 1827.
CROW or CROWE, Nathaniel,
1661.
CRUCIFEX
John, 1712.
Robert, 1689.
Robert, 1745.
CRUMP or CRUMPE
Henry, 1667.
Richard, 1757.
Thomas, 1793.

CRUMPTON, Wilkinson, 1756 (see CROMPTON)
CRUTTENDEN, Thomas, 1677.
CUDWORTH
  Benjamin, 1779.
  William, 1769.
CUE, William, 1691.
CUFFE
  James, 1699.
  John, 1718.
CUMMING, Alexander, 1781.
CUMMON or CUMMINS, Thomas, 1806.
CUNDEE
  Stephen, 1751.
  Stephen, 1797.
CUPER, Josias, 1632.
CURTEEN, William, 1766.
CURTIS
  Elisha, 1766.
  John, 1671.
CUSSINS, Thomas, 1735.
CUTHBERT, Amariah, 1694.
CUTTING, Christopher, 1695.

DALTON, John, 1777.
DANIEL or DANIELL
  Edward, 1647.
  Isaac, 1648.
  Robert, 1708.
  Stephen, 1698.
  Thomas, 1656.
  Thomas, 1773.
  William, 1632.
DANSON, Robert, 1676.
D'ARGENT, James, 1700.
DARLEY or DARNLEY, Matthias, 1759.
DARLING, Robert (Sir), 1740.
DARLOW, Thomas, 1692.
DARTNALL, Thomas, 1713.
DARWELL, Robert, 1708.
DAVENPORT, William, 1706.
DAVERILL, John, 1636.
DAVIS or DAVIES
  Alfred, 1832.
  Benjamin, 1678.
  Charles, 1753.
  George, 1720.
  Henry, 1829.
  James, 1732.
  James, 1803.
  James Robinson, 1881.
  Jeffery, 1690.
  John, 1697.
  John, 1768.
  John, 1818.
  Samuel, 1647.
  Samuel, 1673.
  Simon, 1757.
  Theophilus, 1744.
  Thomas, 1674.
  Thomas, 1757.
  Tobias, 1653.
  William, 1699.
  William, 1774.

William, 1806.
DAVISON
  Richard, 1815.
  William, 1686.
DAWKES, John, 1707.
DAWSON
  John, 1688.
  Robert, 1678.
  Thomas, 1632.
  William, 1778.
DAY
  Edmund, 1692.
  Isaac, 1679.
  John, 1775.
  Thomas, 1691.
DEACON
  Frederick, 1832.
  John, 1781.
  William Archer, 1820.
DEAN, George, 1671.
DEANE
  Phineas, 1734.
  Phineas, 1766.
  Thomas, 1734.
DEARMAR
  Abraham, 1703.
  John, 1680.
  John, 1735.
DEBAUFREE
  James, 1713.
  Peter, 1689.
DE BOUFFLER, Andrew, 1770.
DE CHARMES
  David, 1692.
  Simon, 1691.
DECKA, John, 1757.
DEE, William, 1729.
DE LA FONS
  Henry Peter Burning, 1814.
  John, 1789.
DE LA FOSSE, Samuel, 1692.
DELANDER
  Daniel, 1699.
  James, 1668.
  John, 1675.
  John, 1705.
  John, 1744.
  Nathaniel, 1668.
  Nathaniel, 1721. M.1747.
  Peter, 1641.
DELAUNCE, James, 1677.
DELAVERSPERRE, William, 1650.
DELL, James, 1768.
DENCH, William, 1835.
DENMAN, George Frederick, 1821.
DENNIS
  Francis, 1672.
  John Charles, 1835.
  Peter, 1712.
DENT
  Edmund, 1747.
  Edward John, 1831.
  Robert, 1681.
  William, 1674.

DEPREE, Elie, 1634.
DERRICK, William, 1777.
DE RUMEAUX, Lewis, 1707.
DESBOIS see DUBIOS.
DESBOROUGH, Christopher, 1665.
DESBROW, Robert, 1705.
DESESAR, James, 1707.
DESTACHES, John, 1661.
DEVALL or DAVALL, John, 1677.
DEVIS, John, 1781.
DEWE, John, 1733.
DE WELLKE, Christian, c. 1632. One of the petitioners for incorporation of the Company of Clockmakers.
DIBON, James, 1713.
DICKENS, John, 1688.
DICKINSON, JOHN, 1790.
DIKE, Nathaniel, 1663.
DIMSDALE, John, 1766.
DIMUND, John, 1786.
DINGLEY, Robert, 1668.
DINNIS, Francis (see DENNIS)
DISTURNELL
  Philip, 1769.
  William, 1759.
DITCHFIELD, Richard, 1677
DIXON
  Edward, 1757.
  George James, 1816.
  James, 1789.
  John, 1756.
DOBREE, Robert John, 1863.
DOBSON
  Charles, 1776.
  John, 1714.
  Thomas, 1746.
  William, 1670.
DODD or DODDS
  Alfred, 1847.
  Francis, 1847.
  Joseph, 1794.
  Joseph, 1814.
  Mathew, 1800.
  Philip George, 1834.
DODSWORTH, John, 1648.
DOLLEY
  John, 1804.
  Thomas, 1772. M. 1808.
DOLTON, John, 1784.
DONALD, John, 1771.
DONNE or DON
  Anthony, 1719.
  Robert, 1736.
DOORE, Robert, 1671.
DOOREY, Thomas, 1766.
DORE, Thomas, 1765.
DORMER, James, 1742.
DORRELL or DARRELL
  Francis, 1702.
  Francis, 1755.
  John, 1732.
  William, 1784.

DOSSETT, Gregory, 1662.
DOUGHTY, Tobias, 1696.
DOVE
  Arthur, 1659.
  Henry, 1667.
  Thomas, 1765.
DOWNES
  Christopher, 1632.
  John, 1725.
  John, 1746.
DOWSET, Jeremiah, 1708.
DRAKE, John, c. 1632.
DRAPER
  James, 1712.
  John, 1703.
  John, 1787.
DRAYCOTT, Francis, 1678.
DRAYSEY, John, 1795.
DREW
  Edward, 1692.
  John, 1684.
DROSHOUT, John, 1632.
DROSSATE or DROSADE,
  Samuel, 1675.
DRURY
  James, 1695. M. 1728.
  James, 1751.
  John, 1720.
  John Peter, 1811.
DUBOIS, Jacob, 1730.
DUCASTEL, Isaac, 1703.
DUCHESNE, Claude, 1693.
DUDDS, Joseph, 1732.
DUDSON, Simon, 1654.
DUFF, Robert, 1853.
DUKE
  Joseph, 1682.
  Joseph, 1728.
  Nathaniel, 1663.
DUN, Henry, 1677.
DUNBALL, Richard, 1793.
DUNCOMBE, Richard, 1770.
  M. 1798.
DUNLOP
  Andrew, 1701.
  Conyers, 1733. M. 1758.
DUNN see DUN
  Anthony, 1719.
  Charles, 1773.
  Henry, 1677.
DURANT, Oswald, 1632.
DURDENT, Andrew, 1662.
DUTTON
  Edmund, 1744.
  Mathew, 1779. M. 1800.
  Matthew, 1815.-
  Robert William, 1833.
  Thomas, 1791.
  William, 1746.
DWERRIHOUSE, John, 1781.
DYMOND, John Neate, M.
  1887.
DYSON
  Frank Watson (Sir), M.
  1921 and 1930.
  John, 1695.
EAGLE, John, 1690.

EARLE
  Edward, 1757.
  Thomas, 1720.
EAST
  Edward, 1632. M. 1645
  and 1652.
  Edward, 1710.
  Edward, 1743.
  Edmund or Edward,
  1696.
  Jeremy, 1640.
  John, 1757.
  John, 1765.
  Jordan, 1724.
  Peter, 1692.
  Thomas, 1677.
EASTON or ESTON, Edward,
  1708.
EBSWORTH
  Christopher, 1669.
  John, 1665. M. 1697.
EDEN
  John, 1759.
  William, 1726.
EDENBURY, John, 1791.
EDEY, Richard, 1716.
EDLIN or EDLINE
  Edgar, 1747.
  George, 1810.
  John, 1687.
EDMONDS or EDMUNDS,
  Charles, 1772.
EDRIDGE, William, 1802.
EDWARDS
  George, 1763.
  Isaac, 1719.
  James, 1788.
  James, 1819.
  John, 1775.
  Thomas, 1757.
EDWIN, John, 1743.
EGLETON, Christopher,
  1695.
ELDRED, Dobson, 1782.
ELDRIDGE (see EDRIDGE)
  John, 1677.
  William, 1802.
ELEY, James, 1761.
ELFES, Benjamin, 1674.
ELISHA, Henry, 1928.
ELKES, James, 1819.
ELKINS, William, 1710.
ELLES, Benjamin, 1674.
ELLET, William, 1771.
ELLICOTT
  Edward, 1795. M. 1834
  and 1835.
  John, 1696.
  John, 1782.
ELLIOTT or ELLIOT
  Henry, 1688.
  Henry, 1720.
  Thomas, 1751.
ELLIS
  James, 1667.
  John, 1726.
  John, 1817.
  Paul, 1682.

  Richard, 1683.
  Richard, 1777.
  Richard, 1825.
  Thomas, 1682.
  William James, 1830.
ELLWOOD
  James, 1734.
  John, 1702.
  Martin, 1687.
ELMES
  Richard, 1708.
  Richard, 1747.
  William, 1667.
ELSON, David, 1646.
ELTON
  John, 1675.
  Thomas, 1677.
ELY, Lorkin, 1844.
EMBLEY, Robert Ellis,
  1812.
EMERY
  Josiah, 1781.
  Richard, 1763.
ENYS
  Edward, 1658.
  Edward, 1684.
ERBURY, Henry, 1650.
ERICKE or ERIC
  Robert, 1719.
  William, 1730.
ESTON (see EASTON)
ETHERINGTON, George,
  1684. M. 1709.
ETTY, Marmaduke, 1716.
EVANS
  Dymoke, 1800.
  Henry, 1682.
  James, 1749.
  James, 1811.
  James, 1816.
  John Windus, 1824.
  Samuel, 1822.
  Thomas, 1673.
  Thomas, 1718.
  Thomas, 1720.
  Thomas, 1751.
  Thomas, 1769.
  Thomas, 1783.
EVETT, Robert, 1636.
EXELBY, James, 1718.
EYRE, John, 1703.
EYSTON
  Edward, 1659.
  Thomas, 1651.

FAIRCLOUGH, Thomas,
  1660.
FAIRMAN
  John, 1769.
  Thomas Henry, 1794.
FALCONER, Edward, 1702
  (see FAULKNER)
FAREWELL, John, 1697.
FARMER
  John, 1657.
  Richard, 1683.
  Thomas, 1653.
  Thomas, 1690.

GARON, Peter, 1694.
GARRETT or GARRATT
   Charles, 1690.
   Charles, 1720.
GASCOIGNE, Samuel, 1676.
GASDON, William, 1712.
GASS, William, 1749.
GAUNT, Joseph, 1761.
GAVELL, Benjamin, 1761.
GAVELLE, James, 1683.
GAYDON, Hugh Martin, M.
   1924.
GAZUET, Jerome, 1682.
GELLS, Thomas, 1720.
GEORGE, Richard, 1681.
GERNON, Bernard, 1659.
GIBBONS
   Benjamin, 1729.
   Benjamin, 1750.
   Edward, 1735.
   Harry, 1826.
   Henry, 1838.
   John, 1811.
   Richard, 1730.
GIBBS
   James, 1744.
   John, 1721.
   John, 1736.
   Joshua, 1700.
   Richard, 1815.
   Solomon, 1716.
   Stephen, 1748.
   Thomas, 1681. M. 1711.
   Walter, 1648.
   William, 1707.
GIBSON
   Edward, 1777. M. 1802.
   James, 1669.
   John, 1806.
GIDEON, Robert, 1691.
GIFFIN
   Edward Burr, 1766.
   George, 1740.
GIFFORD, Thomas, 1692.
GILBARD or GILBERT, Faus-
   tin Augustine, 1661.
GILBERT
   Charles, 1700.
   Thomas, 1733.
   William, 1695.
   William, 1767.
   William Henry Sains-
   bury, M. 1904.
GILCHRIST, Archibald,1729.
GILKES, Richard, 1686.
GILL, John, 1707.
GILPIN, Edmund, c. 1632.
   One of the petitioners
   for the incorporation of
   the Company of Clock-
   makers.
GIMINGHAM, John, 1772.
GIROD, James, 1692.
GLADSTONE, Thomas, 1703.
GLAVE, John, 1782.
GLAZIER, William, 1666.
GLENNY
   George, 1819.

   Joseph, 1791.
GLOVER
   Boyer, 1746.
   Daniel, 1699.
   James, 1764.
   John, 1731.
   Richard, 1703.
   Richard, 1733.
   Samuel, 1694.
   Thomas, 1746.
   Thomas, 1767.
GLYNN, Richard, 1705.
GOATER, Robert George,
   1872.
GODBED, William, 1646.
GODDARD
   Benjamin, 1701.
   Christopher, 1756.
   Edward, 1787.
   Isaac, 1684.
   John, 1758.
   William, 1800.
GODDEN, Thomas, 1779.
GODFREY, Henry, 1685.
GOLDSMITH
   John, 1681.
   John, 1720.
   Thomas, 1692.
   William, 1719.
GOOCH, John, 1779.
GOOD or GOODE
   Charles, 1686.
   John, 1678.
   Savil, 1767.
GOODCHILD, John, 1725.
GOODFELLOW,   William
   Richard, 1817.
GOODHALL, William, 1765.
GOODLAD, Richard, 1689.
GOODLIN, Peter, 1637.
GOODYEAR or GOODYER
   John, 1722.
   Joseph, 1732.
GOORE, Thomas, 1716.
GORDIN, John, 1698.
GOSLING, Thomas, 1777.
GOSSE, Jeremiah, 1667.
GOUBERT, James, 1690.
GOUJON
   Samuel, 1763.
   Stephen, 1720. M. 1760.
GOULD
   Abel, 1683.
   Christopher, 1682.
GOWLAND, James, 1831.
GRACE, Edward, 1773.
GRAFTON
   Edward, 1832.
   John, 1830.
GRAHAM, George, 1695. M.
   1722.
GRANGER, Richard, 1695.
GRANT
   Edward, 1769.
   John, 1781.
   John, 1817. M. 1838,
   1839, 1846, 1858 and
   1868.

   Vernor, 1813.
   William, 1660.
GRAPE, Thomas, 1721.
GRATREX, Robert, 1791.
GRAVELL
   Thomas John, 1862.
   William, 1818. M. 1840
   and 1841.
GRAVES
   Benjamin,   1676.   M.
   1705.
   James, 1676.
GRAY
   John, 1769.
   Timothy, 1633.
GREATOREX or GREATORIX
   Henry, 1712.
   Ralph, 1653.
GREEN or GREENE
   Francis, 1772.
   James, 1664.
   James, 1685.
   James, M. 1784.
   James, 1747.
   John, 1712.
   John, 1716.
   John, 1747.
   Joseph, 1723.
   Nathaniel, 1695.
   Samuel, 1772.
   Samuel, 1787.
   William, 1798.
   William, 1815.
GREENFIELD,   William
   Richard, 1814.
GREENWAY
   Joseph, 1747.
   Richard, 1719.
   Richard, 1745.
   William, 1748.
GREGORY
   James, 1657.
   Jeremiah, 1694.
   Jeremy, 1652. M. 1665,
   1666, 1667 and 1676.
   John, 1771.
   Robert, 1678.
   Thomas, 1671.
   Thomas, 1673.
GRENDON, Henry, 1640.
GRETTON, Charles, 1672.
   M. 1700.
GRIBELIN, Simon, 1686.
GRICE, Thomas, 1675.
GRIFFIN or GRIFFEN
   George, 1740.
   George, 1769.
   George, 1827.
   John, 1720.
   Thomas, 1758.
GRIFFITH
   Edward, 1802.
   George, 1720.
   James, 1667.
   Robert, 1706.
   William, 1744.

HAYDEN or HAYDON
  Edward, 1818.
  John, 1784.
  Richard, 1733.
  William, 1687.
  William, 1717.
  William, 1746.
HAYES
  Edmund, 1682.
  Walter, 1654. M. 1680.
HAYNES (see HAINES)
HAYTER, William, 1694.
HAYWARD, William, 1721.
HAYWOOD, John, 1785.
HEADACHE, Thomas, 1784.
HEADDING, Richard William, 1811.
HEADY, George, 1682.
HEARDMAN or HARDMAN
  Jacob, 1721.
  Jacob, 1746.
  John, 1749.
HEARN, Robert, 1834.
HEATH, Thomas, 1762.
HEATHCOTE or HEATHCOCK
  Edward, 1733.
  Timothy, 1698.
HEBB, John, 1736.
HEBERT or HARBART
  Anthony, 1725.
  John, 1682.
  William, 1671.
HECHSTETTER, Joseph,1694.
HEERMAN, John, 1691.
HELDEN or HELDING, Onesiphorus, 1632. One of the petitioners for the incorporation of the Company of Clockmakers.
HELLMAN, James, 1690.
HENSHAW
  John, 1696.
  Walter, 1667. M. 1695.
HENSON, William, 1807.
HERBERT or HARBART
  Cornelius, 1667.
  Cornelius, 1700. M. 1727.
  Cornelius, 1735.
  Edward, 1664.
  Edward, 1711.
  Evan, 1691.
  Henry, 1714.
  John, 1682.
  Thomas, 1676.
  William, 1671.
HERRING, Joseph, 1770.
HESTER
  Henry, 1671.
  Henry, 1689.
HEWARD or HOWARD, John, 1694.
HEWETT or HEWITT
  Alexander, 1725.
  Benjamin, 1724.
  William, 1771.
HEWKLEY
  James Snelling, 1788.

John, 1732.
John, 1775.
Squire, 1741.
Squire, 1764.
HEWSON, John, 1699.
HEYLIN, Isaac, 1795.
HICCOX, John, 1657.
HICKS
  John, 1694.
  Thomas, 1664.
HICKSON, Thomas, 1690.
HIGGINS
  Banger, 1724.
  Thomas, 1735.
  Thomas, 1764.
HIGGINSON
  George, 1736.
  Henry, 1662.
  Samuel, 1698.
HIGGS
  John, 1661.
  John, 1688.
  Peter, 1740. M. 1767.
  Robert, 1714.
  Robert, 1750.
  Thomas, 1716.
HIGHAM, Thomas, 1803.
HIGHMORE, Edward, 1687.
HIGNETT, Richard, 1805.
HILL
  Benjamin, 1640. M.1657.
  Edward, 1698.
  Francis, 1672.
  Francis, 1679.
  John, c. 1630. One of the petitioners for the incorporation of the Company of Clockmakers.
  John, 1670.
  John, 1703.
  John, 1731.
  Sampson Coysgarne, 1795.
  Thomas, 1783.
HILLIAR, Richard, 1740.
HILLIARD or HILLIER
  William, 1679.
  William, 1769.
HILLINGS, Bernard, 1652.
HILLS, John, 1728.
HILTON, John, 1698.
HINDMORE or HINEMORE
  George, 1771.
  John, 1741.
  John, 1777.
HIORNE
  James, 1748.
  John, 1707. M. 1744.
  William, 1741.
HITCHCOCK, John, 1718.
HITCHEN, John, 1720.
HOBART, George, 1717.
HOBBS, Allen, 1734.
HOBLER, Paul, 1781.
HOBSON, John, c. 1630. Petitioner for the incorporation of the

Company of Clockmakers.
HOCHICORN, Isaac, 1728.
HOCKER, John, 1729.
HODDLE, John, 1704.
HODGES
  Samuel, 1770.
  William, 1719.
HOGLATE, John, 1734.
HOLEYARD, Samuel, 1705.
HOLIDAY, Samuel, 1765.
HOLLAND
  George, c. 1630. Petitioner for the incorporation of the Company of Clockmakers.
  Lewis, 1699.
  Thomas, 1632. M. 1656.
  Thomas, 1659.
HOLLIDAIE, Edward, 1650.
HOLLIS, Thomas, 1656.
HOLLOWAY
  Robert, 1632.
  William, 1697.
HOLLYAR or HOLLIARD,
  Samuel, 1705.
HOLMDEN, John George, 1788.
HOLMES
  Matthew Steel, 1817.
  Thomas, 1697.
HOOKE, John, 1698.
HOOPER, Giles, 1758.
HOPCRAFT, Edward, 1734.
HOPKINS
  John, 1640.
  Richard Thomas, 1769.
  Thomas, 1746.
  William, 1751.
HOPPING, James, 1781.
HOPPS, George, 1798.
HORNBLOWER
  Thomas, 1772.
  William, 1714.
  William, 1750.
  William, 1768.
HORNE
  Edward, 1704.
  Henry, 1718. M. 1750.
  Henry, 1820.
  John, 1788.
  Samuel, 1654. M. 1672 and 1673.
HORNSBY, Robert, 1788.
HORSEMAN, Stephen, 1709.
HOTHAM, Henry, 1673.
HOUGHAM (see HUFFAM)
HOUGHTON, Richard, 1690.
HOUNSOM, Thomas, 1746.
HOW or HOWE
  Benjamin, 1691.
  Ephraim, 1729.
  John, 1811.
  Matthew, 1747.
  Samuel, 1712.
  Samuel, 1735.
  Thomas, 1677.
  William, 1667.

HOWARD
John, 1694.
John Jarvis, 1788.
Richard, 1718.
Wharton, 1787.

HOWELL
Benjamin, 1700.
Daniel, 1637.
John, 1724.
Joseph, 1721.

HOWELLS
William, 1780.
William Henry, 1820.

HOWES or HOWSE
Jesse John, 1805.
John, 1672.
John, 1780.
Joseph, 1698.
William, 1730.

HOWKINS, Thomas, 1711.

HOWSE or HOWES
Charles, 1761. M. 1787.
John, 1687.
John, 1707.
Joseph, 1698.
Matthew, 1730.
Thomas, 1632.
William, 1731. M. 1777.

HOWSON, John, 1699.

HOYLE, Henry, 1677.

HUBBARD, John, 1722.

HUBERT
David, 1714. M. 1743.
James, 1712.
Oliver, 1749.

HUCHASON (see HUTCHINSON)

HUE, Pierry (Peter), 1632.

HUFFAM or HOUGHAM
Charles, 1680.

HUGGEFORD, Ignatius, 1671.

HUGHES
John, 1704.
Morris, 1699.
Thomas, 1712. M. 1742.
Thomas, 1742. M. 1765.
William, 1781.

HULL, Henry, 1738.

HULST, Jacob, 1646.

HUMPHREYS or HUMFREYS
Samuel, 1728.
William, 1699.

HUNSDON, William, 1768.

HUNT
Edward, 1684.
James, 1708.
John, 1671.
John, 1699.

HUNTER, Thomas, 1768.

HURLEY
Isaac, 1745.
Jacob, 1765.

HURST
Isaac, 1677.
John, 1771.

HURT
Henry, 1721.

Noe, 1695.

HUSSEY, Joseph, 1685.

HUTCHIN
James, 1698.
John, 1703.
Joseph, 1703.
Joshua, 1683.

HUTCHINSON
Richard, 1702.
William, 1706.

HUTTLY, John, 1788.

HUTTON
Barrett, 1727.
John, 1724.
William, 1762.

HUX, Thomas, 1785.

HYDE, Edward, 1741.

IBELL, Thomas, 1790.

IMLAH, Peter, 1786.

INCHES, Edward James, 1902.

INGLISH, James, 1781.

INGRAM or INGERHAM
Thomas, 1695.
William, 1730.

ION or JON
John, 1811.
Joseph, 1777.

IRELAND
Francis, 1668.
Henry, 1654.

IRVING, Alexander, 1695.

ISACK or ISAAC
Saul, M. 1883.
Sutton, 1662.

IVES
Francis, 1709.
Zachariah, 1682.

IZOD, William, 1649.

JACKSON
Edward, 1669.
Edward, 1680.
Edward, 1790.
James, 1689.
James, 1767.
John, 1682.
John, 1776. M. 1796.
John, 1778.
John, 1779.
John, 1806. M. 1822 and 1826.
John, 1842.
Joseph, 1646.
Joseph, 1746.
Martin, 1697. M. 1721.
Matthew, 1715.
Matthew, 1730.
Richard, 1632.
Thomas, 1688.
William, 1735.
William, 1736.
William, 1739.
William, 1810.
William Henry, 1845.

JACOBS or JACOB
Benjamin, 1706.
Benjamin, 1718.

JAGGAR, Edward, 1702.

JAGGARS, John, 1829.

JAMES
Francis, 1662.
George, 1771.
John, 1661.
Joseph, 1689.
Joseph, 1746.

JAMMETT, Thomas, 1704.

JAQUES
William, 1687. M. 1716.
William, 1724.

JARDIN, John, 1781.

JARMAN, John, 1728.

JARRETT or JARRATT
Barnard, 1787.
George Lewis, 1788.
John William, 1783.
Richard, 1632.
Richard, 1670. M. 1685.

JARVIS
Abel, 1704.
George, 1728.
John, 1762.

JEFFERYS or JEFFERIES
Isaac, 1767.
John, 1639.
John, 1726.
John, 1814.
William Knight, 1712.

JEFFES
Benjamin, 1702.
John, 1697.

JEKYL, Jonathan, 1742.

JELF, William, 1717.

JELLES or JELLY, Thomas, 1720.

JELLISON, Robert, 1736.

JEMMETT
Thomas, 1704.
Thomas, 1803.

JENKINS
Cornelius, 1678.
James, 1692.
Thomas, 1677.
William, 1771.

JENNINGS
Charles, 1725.
Robert, 1703.
Thomas, 1721.

JEPPS, William, 1772.

JERSEY, Francis, 1770.

JEVON
Henry, 1673.
Mary, 1706.

JEYES, James, 1753.

JOHNSON
Charles Jacock, 1750.
Cornelius, 1694.
Edward Daniel, 1859.
George, 1649.
Isaac, 1705.
Isaac, 1723.
Jeremiah, 1668.
John, 1678.

JOHNSON—cont.
John, 1680.
John, 1775.
Michael, 1687.
Roger, 1630. Petitioner
    for the incorporation
    of Company of Clock-
    makers.
Thomas, 1700.
Thomas, 1714.
William, 1702.
William, 1741.
JOHNSTONE, John, 1769.
JOHNSTOUN, James, 1706.
JOLE, Robert, 1667.
JOLLEY or JOLLY
John, 1739.
John, 1777.
Joseph, 1771.
JON see ION
JONES
David, 1687.
Evan, 1647.
Evan Daniel, 1831.
George, 1820.
Henry, 1663. M. 1691.
Henry, 1698.
John, 1716.
John, M. 1762.
John, 1756.
Jonathan, 1687.
Joseph, 1786.
Owen, 1779.
Samuel, 1761.
Thomas, 1679.
Valentine, 1704.
William, 1663.
William, 1759.
William, 1768.
William, 1778.
William Alexander, 1868.
JOSELIN, Edward, 1697.
JOYCE
George, 1692.
Samuel, 1836.
JOYNE, John, 1687.
JULIAN, Gregory, 1664.

KAUS, John, 1712.
KEDDON
Daniel, 1717.
Joshua, 1751.
KEELEY, Thomas, 1784.
KEEN or KEENE
Joseph, 1756.
James Alfred, 1874. M.
    1909.
KELHAM
Joseph, 1766.
Matthais, 1745.
Robert, 1769.
KELLO, Simon, 1723.
KEMM, Samuel, 1763.
KEMP
Charles, 1688.
James, 1780.
Richard, 1701.
William, 1782.

William Henry, 1808.
KEMPS, Matthew, 1670.
KENDRICK
John, 1726.
Roger, 1752.
KENNING, William, 1685.
KENNON, William, 1674.
KENT, Henry, 1640.
KENTON, Joseph, 1686.
KILMINSTER, Henry, 1677.
KING
George, 1831.
Henry, 1721.
Henry Tudor, 1754.
James Frederick, 1808.
John, 1715.
John, 1729.
John, 1753.
John Thomas, 1827.
Jonathan, 1689.
Peter, 1715.
Thomas, 1669.
Thomas, 1699.
Thomas, 1827.
Thomas William, 1802.
William, 1720.
William John, 1720.
KINGSMILL, George, 1667.
KIRBY
Collins, 1758.
Robert, 1723.
Robert, 1741.
KIRK, John, 1677.
KIRTON, John, 1706.
KISSAR, Samuel, 1712.
KNIBB
Joseph, 1670.
Peter, 1677.
Samuel, 1663.
KNIGHT
Charles, 1685.
George, 1780.
Henry, 1723.
Michael, 1681.
Richard, 1682.
KNOTSFORD or KNOTTES-
    FORD, William, 1663.
    M. 1693.
KYNING or KINNING, John,
    1701.

LACEY, William, 1750.
LACY, John, 1722.
LADD
John, Sir, 1820.
Samuel, 1710.
LAIDLAW, Thomas, 1781.
LAING or LAINY, John,
    1720.
LAKE
Bryan, 1674.
Robert, 1770.
LAMB
Edmund, 1676.
James, 1759.
James, 1798.
Thomas, 1632.

LAMBERT
Edward, 1767.
Edward, 1773.
William, 1742.
LAMPE, John, 1714.
LANDIFIELD, Thomas, 1772.
LANE, Josiah, 1736.
LANGCROFT, Richard, 1718.
LANGFORD
Ellis, 1672.
Gowen, 1652.
Thomas, 1781.
William, 1770.
LANGLEY
Cornelius, 1707.
Thomas, 1664.
LASHBROOK or LASH-
    BROOKE
Henry, 1715.
Thomas, 1701.
LATHAM, John, 1700.
LATOUR, René, 1730.
LAW
John, 1768.
Thomas, 1777.
LAWELL (see LOVELL)
LAWLEY, William, M. 1869
    and 1874.
LAWRENCE or LAURENCE
Benjamin, 1779.
Harry, 1796.
Henry, 1704.
LAWSON, John Edward,
    1798.
LAXTON, Thomas, 1642.
LAYTON
Francis, 1726.
John, 1653.
Thomas, 1769.
William, 1710.
LEA, Thomas, 1764. M.
    1782.
LEACH, William, 1749.
LEAF, John, 1785.
LEAKE
Faith, 1685.
George, 1693.
LE CONTE or LE COUNT
Daniel, 1676.
James, 1687.
Peter, 1792.
LEE
Cuthbert, 1676.
James, 1797.
John, 1719.
John, 1737.
John, 1745.
Samuel, 1694.
Sarah, 1756.
Thomas, 1730.
LEEK, John, 1760.
LEEKEY, George, 1778.
LEEMING, Edward, 1766.
LE FEBURE or LEFFEBURE,
    Charles, 1687.
LEFFIN, Thomas, 1720.
LEGG, John, 1724.

MASON
Henry, 1715.
John, 1703.
John, 1712.
John, 1719.
Richard, 1632.
Samuel, 1712.
William, 1688.
MASSEY, Edmund, 1682.
MASSY
Henry, 1692.
Jacob, 1715.
Nicholas, 1682.
Nicholas, 1693.
MASTERS
James, 1809.
William, 1701.
MASTERTON, Richard, 1633.
M. 1642.
MATCHETT, John, 1647.
MATHER
John Bubbers, 1829.
Samuel, 1691.
MATTHEWS
Francis, 1656.
John, 1731.
William, 1731.
William, 1744.
MATTOCKS
John, 1747.
John, 1784.
MAUD
Edward, 1785.
Halstead, 1786.
MAUDUIT, Isaac, 1724.
MAWTASS, Nicholas, 1768.
MAXWELL, Robert, 1778.
MAY
Boys Err, 1754.
Samuel, 1810.
William, 1679.
MAYFIELD, Edward, 1798.
MAYLARD or **MAYLAND**,
Thomas, 1698.
MAYNARD,   Christopher,
1667.
MAYO, Albert Joseph, 1927.
MAYSON (see **MASON**)
MEADES, Thomas, 1687.
MEAN, William, 1789.
MEDHURST, Richard, 1687.
MEIGH, Moses, 1714.
MELVILL, John, 1781.
MERCER, Edward, 1699.
MERCHANT (see **MARCHANT**)
MEREDITH
John, 1664.
Lancelot, 1637.
MERFIELD, William, 1825.
MERIGEOT, John, 1750.
MERRILL
Charles, 1757.
Charles, 1782.
John, 1777.
MERRY
Charles, 1735. M. 1768.
Edward, 1749.
James Owen, 1771.

MERRYMAN or **MERRIMAN**
Benjamin, 1682.
Henry, 1674.
John, 1711.
MERTTINS,   George,   Sir,
1688. M. 1713.
MESNIEL, James, 1682.
MESTAYER
Henry, 1713.
Henry, 1744.
METCALFE, George Mar-
maduke, 1781.
MICHEL, Edward Eccott,
1831.
MICHINALE (see **MITCHIN-
ALLE**)
MICKLEWRIGHT
Erasmus, 1673.
Erasmus James, 1708.
MIDDLETON,   Timothy,
1687.
MIDNALL, John, 1632.
MIDWINTER
Thomas, 1774.
William, 1774.
MILBORNE, John, 1698.
MILES
John Henry, 1875.
Septimus, 1797.
Thomas, 1768.
MILLER
John, 1674.
Joseph, 1728.
Peter, 1681.
Ralph, 1697.
William, 1743.
MILLETT
Edward, 1680.
William, 1715.
MILLION, William, 1671.
MILLIS, Michael, 1736.
MILLON, Daniel, 1712.
MILLS
Ralph, 1697.
Robert, 1772.
Robert, 1838.
Thomas, 1652.
Thomas, 1766.
MILNER
Thomas, 1739.
Thomas, 1763.
MILTON, Thomas, 1777.
MINCHIN, John, 1789.
MINUEL, David, 1683.
MIRFIELD, Robert, 1749.
MISON (see **MYSON**)
MITCHELL
James Edward, 1829.
John, 1713.
John, 1751.
Myles, 1640.
Robert, 1766.
MITCHINALLE,   William,
1702.
MITFORD
John, 1710.
Robert, 1738.
Robert, 1773.

MOLTON (see **MOULTON**)
MOLYNS, Charles, 1709.
MONDAY   or   **MUNDAY**,
Joseph, 1654.
MOODYE, David, 1649.
MOON
Christopher, 1768.
William, 1808.
MOORE
Daniel, 1697.
Edward, 1732.
Edmund Thomas, 1781.
George, 1856. M. 1870
and 1875.
John, 1744.
Joseph, 1690.
William, 1701.
William, 1759.
MORELAND or **MORLAND**
John, 1738.
John, 1766.
MORELLEY or **MORALEY**,
William, 1688.
MORGAN
Edward, 1735.
Henry, 1677.
John, 1704.
John, 1790.
Jude, 1654.
Richard, c. 1630. Peti-
tioner for incorporation
of Company of Clock-
makers.
Robert, 1647.
Thomas, 1659.
Walter, 1847.
William, 1658.
William, 1704.
MORICE, David, 1796.
MORLEY, William., 1703.
MORRIS, Edward, 1672.
MORRIT, William, 1769.
MORT, John, 1762.
MOSELEY
Elinor, 1726.
William, 1680.
MOSS, Thomas, 1786.
MOTLEY, Richard, 1682.
MOTT or **MOTH**, Thomas,
1656.
MOTTEUX, Samuel, 1697.
MOULTON
Edward, 1773.
Thomas, 1796.
MOUNT
Edward, 1731.
William, 1692.
MOUNTFORD,   Zachariah,
1684.
MOWRY, Anthony, 1766.
MOWTLOW
Conon, 1700.
Henry, 1685.
Henry, 1715.
Henry, 1749.
MUCKARSIE or **MACKARSIE**
George James, 1814.
James, 1784.

PATCHING, Elisha, 1728.
PATMORE, Peter, 1813.
PATRICK
  John, 1712.
  Thomas, 1765.
PATTEE, Thomas, 1793.
PATTENSON or PATTISON,
  Robert, 1668.
PAUL
  Thomas, 1670.
  William, 1766.
PAWLET, John, 1740.
PAYNE
  Nicholas, 1648.
  Richard, 1725.
  Southerne, 1750. M.
  1778.
PEACHEY
  James, 1783.
  John, 1755.
  Newman, 1749.
  William, 1728.
  William, 1754.
PEARCE or PEIRCE
  Adam, 1664.
  Henry, 1749.
  William, 1786. M. 1804.
PECK
  Floyd, 1753.
  George, 1725.
  George, 1755.
PECKETT, John, 1691.
PEIRCE, see PEARCE and
  PIERCE
PENFOLD, Joshua, 1695.
PENKETHMAN, Thomas,
  1692.
PENN
  John, 1764.
  Thomas, 1776.
PENNOCK
  John, 1638. M. 1660 and
  1663.
PENNY
  John, 1770.
  John, 1804.
PEPPER, Thomas, 1764.
PEPYS
  John, 1680. M. 1707.
  John, 1715. M. 1739.
  Richard, 1674.
  William, 1723.
PERCIVAL, William Chen-
  nel, 1822.
PERES, Mark, 1680.
PERIGAL
  Francis, 1741. M. 1756.
  Francis, 1756. M. 1775.
  Francis S., 1781. M.
  1806.
  Francis, 1786.
  John, 1781.
PERKINS
  James, 1730.
  Richard George, 1847.
PERRY or PERREY
  Henry, 1691.
  John, 1691.

John Aldington, 1807.
  M. 1850 and 1851.
  Joseph, 1814.
  Peter, 1763.
  Peter, 1784.
PETER, Richard, 1679.
PETIT, Guillaume, c. 1630.
  One of the petitioners
  for the incorporation of
  the Company of Clock-
  makers.
PETRE, James, 1770.
PETTY, William, 1646.
PEW, Edward Phillips,
  1778.
PEYTLING, Thomas, 1682.
PHAREZ, John, 1774.
PHILLIPS
  Charles, Thomas, 1819.
  James, 1772.
  Jonas, 1771.
  Philip, 1777.
  Philip, 1832.
PHIPPS, James, 1767.
PICKNETT, Joseph, 1771.
PIERCE or PEIRCE
  Humphrey, 1653.
  Richard, 1657.
  Zacharias, 1788.
PIERRE, Pasquier, 1648.
PIGOTT, Henry, 1687.
PINCHBECK, Christopher,
  1781.
PINE, Philip, 1775.
PINNELL, William, 1735.
PIPER, Thomas, 1752.
PISTOR, Edward, 1777.
PITAN, James, 1748.
PITCHER, John, 1689.
PITMAN, John, 1714.
PITNEY, Thomas, 1759.
PITT
  Thyar, 1784.
  William, 1775.
PLANNER
  Thomas, 1701.
  Thomas, 1730.
PLANT, Edward, 1664.
PLATT, Thomas, 1637.
PLAYER
  Robert, 1678.
  Robert, 1700.
  Thomas, 1672.
PLEUVIER, Isaac, 1652.
PLUETT, Anthony, 1697.
PLUMER, Thomas, 1701
  (see PLANNER)
PLUMLEY
  Charles, 1819.
  William, 1756. M. 1779.
  William, 1780. M. 1801.
PLUMPTON, James, 1763.
POMROY or POMEROY
  Joseph, 1728.
  Joseph, 1757.
POOLE
  Edmund, 1722.
  George, 1654.

James, 1778.
John, 1743.
Matthew, 1794.
Robert, 1754. M. 1781.
William, 1777.
PORTER
  Francis, 1730.
  John, 1779.
  Matthew, 1692.
  Samuel, 1756.
  William, 1771.
POST, Richard, 1771.
POTTER
  Christopher, 1730.
  Harry, 1778. M. 1795.
  Harry, 1792. M. 1812.
  James, 1809.
  William, 1738.
POULINGUE
  Jacob, 1781.
  John, 1743.
POULSON, William, 1801.
POWELL
  Bartholomew, 1668.
  Edward, 1777.
  Robert, 1710.
  William, 1763.
POWER, Anne, 1722.
PRENTICE, Philip, 1749.
PRESTIDGE, Bartholomew,
  1704.
PRESTON, Edward, 1721.
PRESTWOOD, Joseph, 1703.
PRETTY, John, 1807.
PRICE
  David, 1770.
  Francis, 1786.
  George, 1772.
  John, 1744.
  Richard, 1772.
PRIDDITH, Thomas, 1639.
PRIEST
  John, 1746.
  Thomas, 1729.
PRIGG, John, 1732.
PRIME
  Abraham, 1672.
  Andrew, 1646.
  Andrew, 1736.
PRINCE, Richard, 1680.
PRINT, Richard, 1698.
PROCTOR, William, 1797.
PUCKRIDGE
  Charles, 1776.
  John, 1788.
PUGH, Benjamin, 1777.
PULBROOK, Joseph Zacha-
  riah, 1822.
PULLEN or PULLIN
  Charles, 1745.
  David, 1745.
  David, 1773.
PULLER, Jonathan, 1683.
PURDIN, John, 1777.
PURRIER, Richard, 1706.
PUTLEY, Francis, 1804.
PUZY, Isaac, 1658.

PYKE
George, 1753.
John, 1720.
PYM, Thomas, 1721.
PYNE, Nathaniel, 1677.

QUARE, Daniel, 1671. M. 1708.
QUASH, Joseph, 1646.
QUINTON, William Brett, 1769.

RADFORD
Henry, 1722.
Thomas, 1749.
RAGER, James, 1769.
RAINES, William, 1660.
RAINIER
Daniel, 1806.
John, 1786.
RAINSFORD
Barnard, 1677.
Benjamin, 1708.
Francis, 1689.
John, 1721.
RAKE, John, 1780.
RAMSAY
David, the first master of the Company of Clockmakers, 1632.
John, 1637.
RAMSDEN, Thomas, 1648.
RAMSEY, John, 1637. (Same as RAMSAY.)
RANCEFORD, Barnard, 1677 (see RAINSFORD).
RANSOM, Robert Hill, 1777.
RANT
John, 1687.
Jonathan, 1687.
RAPSON, John Stewart, 1773.
RASHER, Joseph, 1703.
RAVEN, Samuel, 1768.
RAVES, Charles, 1768.
RAWLINS or **RAWLINGS**
Charles, 1818.
Henry, 1706.
James, 1775.
RAYMENT, Thomas, 1719.
RAYNER
Dove, 1701.
John, 1697.
Stephen, 1691.
READING
Daniel, 1743.
Robert, 1761.
REDKNAP, Enos, 1792.
REED or **REID**
Alexander, 1707.
George Jeremiah, 1816.
William, 1824.
REEVE
Garvess, 1730.
Henry, 1682.
John, 1712.
Thomas, 1632.
REGARD, Reymond, 1677.

REID (see **REED**), Thomas, 1825.
REITH, James, 1706.
REWALLING, Thomas, 1715.
REYNOLDS
James, 1766.
Joseph, 1691.
Thomas, 1706.
Thomas, 1736.
RHODENHURST, William, 1776.
RHODES, William, 1762.
RIBOULEAU, Lason, 1746.
RICE, Thomas, 1800.
RICHARD, Peter, 1679.
RICHARDS
Henry, 1699.
Hugh, 1709. M. 1735.
James, 1770.
Luke, 1646.
Richard, 1652.
RICHARDSON
Charles, 1739.
Charles, 1760.
Henry, 1813.
James, 1770. M. 1788.
John, 1738.
John, 1807.
Richard, 1675.
Thomas Kealley, 1775.
RICKARD, John, 1657.
RICORD, Richard, 1649.
RIDDLESON, Samuel, 1766.
RIDER, Thomas, 1698.
RIDLEY, Josiah, 1685.
RIGBY, Joshua, 1781.
RILEY (see **RYLEY**), James, 1752.
RING, John, 1693.
RIPPON, William Frederick, 1831.
RISOLIERE, Isaac, 1756.
RIVERS
David, 1753.
David, 1766. M. 1773.
David, 1789.
Thomas, 1784.
William, 1770. M. 1794.
William, 1776.
RIVIERE, Jacob, 1756.
ROACH, Thomas, 1852.
ROBERTS
Hugh, 1664.
John, 1771.
John, 1776,
John, 1805.
ROBINS
Joshua, 1808.
Thomas, 1774.
William, 1779. M. 1805, 1813 and 1814.
ROBINSON
Francis, 1707. M. 1725.
George, 1631.
Henry, 1733.
Joseph, 1769.
Martin, 1812.
Oliver, 1727.

Robert, 1652.
Ruhamah, 1713.
Samuel, 1785.
Thomas, 1703.
Thomas, 1812.
William, 1667.
William, 1720.
ROBSON, William, 1787. M. 1809, 1816 and 1818.
ROGERS
Charles, 1657.
Isaac, 1776. M. 1813 and 1824.
John, 1732.
Thomas, 1763.
Thomas, 1820.
William, 1640.
ROGERSON
Joshua, 1773.
William, 1754. M. 1774.
ROMER, Isaac, 1661.
ROMLEY, Christopher, 1755
ROMNEY, Joseph, 1664.
ROOF, Daniel, 1676.
ROOKE, John, 1781.
ROOKER
Richard, 1694.
Richard, 1729.
ROOKES, Barlow, 1665.
ROSE
John, 1748.
Michael, 1676.
William, 1767.
ROSSE, Samuel, 1672.
ROTHERHAM
Hugh, M. 1925.
Thomas, 1662.
ROTHWOOD
Robert, 1632.
Robert, 1646.
ROULEAU, Benjamin, 1777.
ROULLET, Gabriel, 1753.
ROUMIEU
Adam, 1687.
Adam, 1727.
James, 1692.
John, 1720.
Lewis de, 1707.
ROUND
George, 1826.
Martin Carr, 1832.
ROUNDELL, Thomas, 1749.
ROWDEN, 1691.
ROWE
Benjamin, 1708.
George, 1739.
Thomas, 1699.
ROWLAND or **ROWLANDS**
Christopher, 1810.
William, 1820. M. 1860 and 1867.
ROWLEY
James, 1721.
John, 1793.
ROY, David, 1682.
ROYCROFT, Thomas, 1699.
ROYD, Stephen Joseph, 1767.

SWINNY, Henry, 1773.
SWIRRIHOUSE, John, 1781.
SYLVESTER (see SILVESTER)
SYMONDS, Richard, 1691.
SYMONS, Thomas, 1661.

TALBOYS, Jacob, 1763.
TALLIS, Aaron, 1722.
TANNER, Joseph, 1682.
TARLES, John, 1690.
TARRANT, William, 1821.
TAWNEY, James, 1759.
TAYLOR
    Abraham, 1668.
    Benjamin, 1773.
    Charles, 1723.
    Edward, 1645.
    Edward, 1800.
    Henry Cleaver, 1746.
    James, 1802.
    Jasper, 1695.
    Jasper, 1729. M. 1754.
    John, 1687.
    John, 1702.
    Richard, 1655.
    Richard, 1724.
    Robert, 1703.
    Samuel, 1770. M. 1807.
    Samuel, 1830.
    Thomas, 1646. M. 1668, 1669 and 1687.
    Thomas, 1659.
    Thomas, 1685. M. 1710.
    William, 1682.
    William, 1753.
TEBBATT, Benoni, 1683.
TEMPLE, Thomas, 1720.
TEMPLER, Charles, 1673.
TENNANT, Thomas, 1668.
TERRIER
    James, 1694.
    Mary, 1714.
    Thomas, 1694.
TETLEY, James, 1794.
THACHE
    Philip, 1685.
    Robert, 1689.
THOMACQUE or THOME-
    GUEX, Abraham, 1676.
THOMAS
    Daniel, 1682.
    Daniel Jenkin, 1894.
    William, 1772.
THOMASON,   Troughton, 1732.
THOMPSON
    Edward John, 1860. M. 1885 and 1894.
    Henry, 1748.
    Isaac, 1699.
    Jeremiah, 1770.
    John, 1662.
    John, 1720.
    John Littler, 1812.
    Richard, 1673.
    Robert, 1681.
    Troughton,   1732   (see THOMASON)

William, 1708.
THORNTON
    Henry, 1699.
    John, 1731.
    William, 1792.
THOROWGOOD or THORO-
    GOOD
    Edward, 1668.
    Frederick, 1810.
    John, 1660.
    Luke, 1768.
    William, 1660.
THORP or THORPE
    Edward, 1780.
    John, 1657.
    Thomas, 1820.
THWAITES
    Aynsworth, 1751.
    Benjamin, 1770.
    John, 1782. M. 1815, 1819 and 1820.
THWING (see TWHING)
TICHBOURN, John, 1771.
TIGHT, George, 1791.
TILLY, Joseph, 1704.
TIPPING, George, 1674.
TITCHENER,   Benjamin, 1763.
TITFORD, John, 1723.
TODD
    Benjamin, 1747.
    John, 1707.
TOLBY, Charles, 1720.
TOLLER
    Bostock, 1766.
    Thomas, 1741.
TOLLEY
    Charles, 1683.
    Charles, 1720.
TOLSON
    John, 1715.
    Ralph, 1701.
TOMKINS or TOMPKINS
    William, 1762.
    William, 1819.
TOMLIN, Edward, 1768.
TOMLINS, Nicholas, 1646.
TOMLINSON
    George, 1673.
    William, 1699. M. 1733.
TOMPION
    Thomas, 1671. M. 1703.
    Thomas, 1702.
TORADO, Francis, 1633.
TOTHAKER, William, 1703.
TOURLE, William, 1776.
TOWLE, Edward, 1760.
TOWNESEN
    Samuel, 1702.
    William, 1716.
TREGENT, James, 1781.
TRENHOLME, William, 1728.
TRIGG, Thomas, 1701.
TRIGGS, Thomas, 1708.
TRIPPETT
    John, 1668.
    Robert, 1700.
    William, 1706.

TROUGHTON, Thomas, 1796.
TROVEY, Charles, 1776.
TROW, Gilbert, 1722.
TRUBSHAW, John, 1686.
TRUSTY, Stephen, 1770.
TUCKEY, Thomas, 1646.
TUNNELL, John, 1826.
TUNSTALL, John, 1852.
TURGES, Josias, 1764.
TURNELL, William, 1828.
TURNER
    Charles, 1785.
    Charles Thomas, 1811.
    Edward, 1769.
    James, 1801.
    Joseph, 1717.
    Thomas, 1735.
    William, 1821.
TUTET, Edward, 1765. M. 1786.
TUTTLE, Thomas, 1695.
TWHING, James, 1688.
TWYFORD, Robert, 1781.
TYLER, George, 1699.
TYRELL, Walter, 1740.

UFFINGTON
    George, 1728.
    John, 1702.
    John, 1739.
    Samuel, 1740.
ULYATE, William, 1773.
UNDERHILL
    Benjamin, 1785.
    Cave, 1655.
UNDERWOOD
    William, 1759.
UPJOHN
    Francis, 1781.
    James, 1781.

VALENTINE
    Charles Davis Frederick, 1809.
    John, 1771.
VANLOVE, Matthew, 1692.
VANSCOLINAR,   Jeremiah, 1776.
VASEY, John, 1766.
VASLET, Andrew, 1717.
VASSIERE, Thomas, 1698.
VAUGHAN, Edward, 1715.
VECUE, Thomas, 1632.
VENABLES
    George, 1769.
    George, 1795.
VENN, Thomas, 1772.
VERNON
    Samuel, 1648. M. 1679.
    Samuel, 1685.
    Thomas, 1708.
VICK, Richard, 1702. M. 1729.
VIELL, Charles, 1686.
VIET, Claude, 1698.
VIGNE, James, 1781.
VIGNEAU, Peter, 1709.

VINE
Thomas Walter, 1892.
George Henry Misban, 1901.
VINER, Charles Edward, 1813.
VINN, Thomas, 1772.
VIRGOE, Thomas, 1682.
VOLANT, Elias, 1632.
VOYCE, Gamaliel, 1694.
VULLIAMY
Benjamin, 1781.
Benjamin Lewis, 1809. M. 1821, 1823, 1825, 1827 and 1847.
Justin Theodore, 1813.

WADE
Burtt, 1764.
Henry, 1728.
Henry, 1768..
WAINEWRIGHT, John, 1679.
WAKELING, Samuel, 1767.
WAKER (perhaps WALKER), Peter, 1663.
WALBANK or WALLBANK
William, 1767.
William, 1796.
WALDOE, John, 1677.
WALDRON, John, 1763.
WALFORD
John, 1717.
Thomas, 1690.
WALKDEN, Thomas, 1694.
WALKER
George, 1684.
Jonadab, 1687.
Jonah, 1734.
John, 1632.
John, 1717.
John, 1771.
John, 1788.
Joseph, 1787.
Samuel, 1766.
Thomas, 1803.
William, 1759.
William, 1764.
WALL, John, 1809.
WALLBANK (see WALBANK)
WALLEN, William, 1738.
WALLIS, William, 1716.
WALLITT, Richard, 1693.
WALTER or WALTERS
John, 1645.
Nicholas, c. 1630. Subscriber to incorporation of Company of Clockmakers.
WANOSTROCHT or WONOSTROCHT, Vincent, 1804.
WARBURTON, William, 1693.
WARD
Edward, 1638.
Edward, 1732.
John, 1730.
John, 1772. M. 1797.
Robert, 1778.
Thomas, 1632.

William, 1767.
William, 1800.
William, 1845.
WARDEN, Samuel, 1785.
WARE, Robert, 1701.
WARFIELD, Alexander, 1692.
WARHAM, William, 1773.
WARNER
John, 1682.
John, 1696.
WARREN
Richard, 1668.
Thomas, 1803.
WATERS
John, 1682.
Robert, 1767.
Thomas, 1732.
WATKINS
George, 1716.
John, 1787.
John, 1810.
WATSON
Alexander, 1742.
Edward, 1704.
Edward, 1815.
Edward, 1854.
John, 1744.
John, 1781.
Samuel, 1687.
Walter, 1719.
William, 1691.
William, 1813.
WATTERS, Thomas, 1732.
WATTES, John, 1664.
WATTS
Brouncker, 1693.
James, 1720.
John, 1712.
Richard, 1680.
Robert, 1785.
Walter, 1695.
WAUGH, John, 1804.
WAYLETT
James, 1769.
John, 1794.
WEAVER
Cuthbert, 1682.
Francis, 1748.
George, 1740.
WEBB
Ambrose, 1721.
Benjamin, 1781.
Isaac, 1668.
Thomas, 1789.
WEBSTER
George, 1703.
Henry, 1710.
Henry, 1742.
John, 1695.
Percy, M. 1926.
Richard, 1779.
Richard, 1807.
Richard, 1844.
Robert, 1675. M. 1704.
Samuel, 1756.
Thomas, 1709.
William, 1710.

William, 1734. M. 1755.
William, 1763.
WEEDON, William, 1695.
WEEKES or WEEKS
Charles, 1713.
Johnson, 1683.
Thomas, 1654.
WELLBORNE
Charles, M. 1873 and 1880.
William, 1783.
WELCH, William, 1811.
WELCOME, John, 1705.
WELLER, John, 1713.
WELLINGTON, John, 1726.
WELLS
George, 1832.
John, 1682.
Joseph, 1668.
William, 1689.
WENTWORTH, George, 1738.
WESCOTT, John, 1703.
WEST
Jacob, 1757.
James, 1741.
Samuel, 1766.
Thomas, 1695.
Thomas, 1698.
William, 1698.
William, 1782.
WESSTEN or WESTON, Robert, 1721.
WESTOBY, John, 1677.
WESTWOOD, Richard, 1691.
WHATLEY, Robert, 1821.
WHATSON (see WATSON)
WHEATLEY
John, 1668.
William, 1698.
WHEELER
John, 1680.
Thomas, 1655. M. 1684.
William, 1774.
WHICHCOTE
Samuel, 1724. M. 1748.
Samuel, M. 1764.
WHITAKER, Edward, 1712.
WHITE
Amos, 1741.
Cæsar, 1692.
John, 1646.
John, 1670.
John, 1692.
Joseph, 1714.
Thomas, 1683.
WHITEAVES, Richard, 1788.
WHITEBREAD, William, 1728.
WHITEHEAD, Richard, 1671.
WHITEHURST, John, 1851.
WHITFIELD, Edward, 1663.
WHITFORD, Thomas, 1768.
WHITLATCH, John, 1637.
WHITLOCK
James, 1704.
James, 1744.
WHITLOW, Searle, 1826.
WHITTLE, Thomas, 1683.

WHITTON
Clay, 1698.
Richard, 1740.
WHITWELL, Robert, 1649.
WICHELL, Samuel, 1705.
WICKENS, John, 1755.
WICKES
Alfred Nelson, 1833.
John, 1784.
John Haughton, 1807.
Joseph, 1794.
WICKS, William, 1771.
WIGHTMAN
George, 1738.
James, 1670.
Thomas, 1701.
William, 1696.
WIGHTWICK, John, 1781.
WIGSON, William, 1781.
WILCOCKS, Daniel, 1757.
WILD, Thomas, 1766.
WILDER
John, 1790.
Richard, 1776.
WILKINS
Jonathan, 1754.
Robert, 1670.
Speed, 1704.
William, 1784.
WILKINSON
William, 1718.
William, 1749.
WILLANS, William, 1807.
WILLCOCKS, Richard, 1782.
WILLIAMS
Alexander, 1790.
Charles, 1771.
George, 1801.
John, 1753.
John, 1768.
John, 1792.
John, 1796.
John, 1815.
WILLIAMSON
John, 1682.
John Henry, 1866.
Joseph, M. 1724.
Michael, 1714.
Robert, 1666. M. 1698.
Thomas, 1668.
William, 1663.
WILLIAMSTON, Ralph, 1706.
WILLIARME, Pierre, 1648.
WILLIN, William, 1807.
WILLIS, Richard Ockshutt, 1760.
WILLOUGHBY
John, 1686.
John, 1711.
WILLOWE, John, 1632. M. 1635.
WILLS, John, 1770.
WILMOT or WILLMOT
George, 1670.
Stephen, 1674.
Thomas, 1716.

WILSON or WILLSON
Alexander, 1781.
Charles, 1824.
Edward, 1670.
George, 1692.
George, 1730.
James, 1723.
James, 1781.
John, 1784.
Robert, 1733.
Thomas, 1659.
Thomas, 1807.
William, 1693.
WINCH, Amos, 1677.
WINDMILLS
Joseph, 1671. M. 1702.
Thomas, 1695. M. 1719.
WINDOW, Daniel, 1718.
WINDSOR, James, 1787.
WING, William, 1860. M. 1872 and 1879.
WINNOCK
Daniel, 1708.
Joshua, 1672.
WINROW, William, 1718.
WINSMORE
John, 1712.
William, 1712.
WIRRALL, Copley, 1647.
WISE or WYSE
John, 1646.
John, 1669.
John, 1683.
John, 1710.
Joseph, 1687.
Luke, 1694.
Mark, 1719.
Peter, 1693. M. 1725.
Richard, 1679.
Robert, 1695.
Thomas, 1686.
WISEMAN, John, 1646.
WITCHELL, Robert, 1744.
WITHER, John, 1699.
WITHERS, John, 1790.
WITTE, Samuel, 1660.
WIWEL, Christian Henry, 1823.
WOGDEN, Stephen, 1724.
WOLVERSTONE or WOL-FRESTON
Benjamin, 1656.
James, 1677.
Thomas, 1650.
WONTNER
John, 1770.
John, 1807.
WOOD
Bartholomew, 1780.
Henry, 1720.
James, 1745.
John, 1701.
Robert, 1671.
Thomas, 1691.
Thomas, 1727.
William, 1755.

WOODALL
Edward, 1807.
Thomas, 1796.
WOODDEN, Charles, 1755.
WOODS, Thomas, 1714.
WOODWARD, Joseph, 1820.
WOOLFE, John, 1728.
WORTHINGTON
Basil, 1752.
John, 1721.
John, 1746.
WRAGG, Houblon, 1724.
WRAY, Hilton, 1769. M. 1785.
WRENCH
Charles, 1785.
Charles James, 1814.
WRIGHT
Benjamin, 1685.
George, 1720.
James, 1733
John, 1661.
John, 1671.
John, 1696.
John, 1700.
John, 1715.
John, 1781.
Robert, 1634.
Thomas, 1770.
William, 1817.
William, 1891.
WRIGHTSON, Thomas, M. 1737.
WROTH, Edward, 1797.
WYCH, David, 1694.
WYER, Joseph, 1770.
WYETH, John, 1655.
WYLDER, John, 1790 (see WILDER)
WYNN or WYNNE
Henry, 1662. M. 1690.
John, 1678.
Richard, 1773.
WYRALL (see WIRRALL)
WYTHE, Lionel, 1645.

YATES
Samuel, 1647.
Samuel, 1685.
YEATMAN, Andrew, 1692.
YEOMANS, Ralph, 1722.
YORKE
Joseph Wadham, 1742.
Thomas, 1716.
Thomas, 1799.
YOUNG or YOUNGE
Henry, 1672.
James, 1786.
Robert, 1747.
Thomas, 1699.
William, 1668.
William, 1682.
William, 1801.

ZACHARY, John, 1694.

BIBLIOGRAPHY

ATKINS, CHARLES EDWARD: *Register of Apprentices of the Worshipful Company of Clockmakers.* 1931.

BAILLIE, G. H.: *Watchmakers and Clockmakers of the World.* 2nd ed. 1947.

BRITTEN, F. J.: *Old Clocks and Watches and their Makers.* 6th ed. 1932.

BRITTEN, F. W.: *Horological Hints and Helps.* 2nd ed. 1934.

CESCINSKY, H.: *Old English Master Clockmakers and their Clocks.* 1938.

CESCINSKY, H., and WEBSTER, M.R.: *English Domestic Clocks.* 1913.

COLE, T. W.: *Origin and Use of Church Scratch Dials.* 1935. (Pamphlet.)

DERHAM, WILLIAM: *The Artificial Clock-maker.* 1696. 4th ed. 1759.

EDEN, H. K. E., and LLOYD, E.: *The Book of Sundials.* 1900.

Enclyclopædia Britannica: Articles on Clocks, Dials and Equation of Time.

GORDON, G. F. C.: *Clockmaking, Past and Present.* 1925.

HOPE-JONES, F.: *Electrical Timekeeping.* 1940.

REID, THOMAS: *Clock and Watch Making.* 1846.

SMITH, JOHN: *Horological Dialogues.* 1675. *Horological Disquisitions.* 1694.

TIMBS, JOHN: *Wonderful Inventions.* 1882.

WOOD, E. J.: *Curiosities of Clocks and Watches* 1866.

WORCESTER, MARQUIS OF: *Century of Inventions.* 1663. 7th ed. 1825.

WARD, F. A. B.: *Handbook of the collections Illustrating Time Measurement: Science Museum.*

BOOKS RELATING TO AMERICAN CLOCKMAKING

CHANDLEE, EDWARD E.: *Six Quaker Clockmakers.* 1943.

DREPPERD, CARL W.: *American Clocks and Clockmakers.* 1947.

HOOPES, PENROSE: *Connecticut Clockmakers of the Eighteenth Century.*

JEROME, CHAUNCEY: *History of the American Clock Business.* 1860.

MOORE, N. HUDSON: *The Clock Book.* 1911.

WILLARD, JOHN WARE: *A History of Simon Willard, Clockmaker.* 1911.

INDEX

Page references to illustrations in italics